IQ and Aptitude Tests
Assess your verbal, numerical and spatial reasoning skills

Philip Carter

LONDON PHILADELPHIA NEW DELHI

First published in Great Britain and the United States in 2007 by Kogan Page Limited
This edition 2011

120 Pentonville Road	525 South 4th Street, #241	4737/23 Ansari Road
London N1 9JN	Philadelphia PA 19147	Daryaganj
United Kingdom	USA	New Delhi 110002
www.koganpage.com		India

© Philip Carter 2007, 2011

ISBN   978 0 7494 6195 9
E-ISBN   978 0 7494 6199 7

British Library Cataloguing-in-Publication Data

A CIP record for this book is available from the British Library.

Library of Congress Cataloging-in-Publication Data

Carter, Philip J.
     IQ and aptitude tests : assess your verbal, numerical and spatial reasoning skills / Philip Carter.
          p. cm.
     ISBN 978-0-7494-6195-9 – ISBN 978-0-7494-6199-7 (e-bk)   1. Intelligence tests.
2. Ability–Testing.   3. Self-evaluation.   I. Title.   II. Title: Intelligence quotient and aptitude tests.
     BF431.3.C3617 2011
     153.9′3–dc22

                                                                              2010031004

Typeset by Graphicraft Ltd, Hong Kong
Printed and bound in India by Replika Press Pvt Ltd

Contents

Introduction

An aptitude test is, generally, any test designed to measure potential for achievement.

The word *aptitude* is sometimes misused to mean 'ability' or 'achievement'; however, there is a subtle difference between the three words *aptitude*, *ability* and *achievement*, which can be distinguished as follows:

- *aptitude* – how quickly or easily you will be able to learn in the future;

- *ability* – what you are able to demonstrate in the present;

- *achievement* – what you have accomplished in the past.

There are nine different types of aptitude, which may be summarized as follows:

- *General learning:* learning and understanding, reasoning and making judgements. Example: how well we achieve at school.

- *Verbal aptitude:* general lexical skills – understanding words and using them effectively.

- *Numerical aptitude:* general mathematical skills – working with numbers quickly and accurately.

- *Spatial aptitude:* understanding geometric forms, and the understanding and identification of patterns and their meaning. Example: understanding how to construct a flat-pack piece of furniture from a set of instructions.

- *Form perception:* inspecting and perceiving details in objects, and making visual comparisons between shapes. Examples: studying an object under a microscope, and quality inspection of goods.

- *Clerical perception:* reading, analysing and obtaining details from written data or tabulated material. Examples: proof-reading, analysing reports and understanding graphs.

- *Motor coordination:* eye and hand coordination, and making quick and accurate rapid movement responses. Examples: actually being able to assemble the flat-pack piece of furniture once you have understood how it should be done, being able to operate a computer keyboard quickly and accurately, and sporting skills.

- *Finger dexterity:* manipulating small objects quickly and accurately. Examples: playing a musical instrument, and sewing.

- *Manual dexterity:* the skill of being able to work with your hands. Examples: painting and decorating, building things and operating machinery.

In the case of most aptitude tests there is usually a set time limit, which must be strictly adhered to in order for the test to be valid, and there is usually an average score that has been standardized in comparison with the scores of a group of people who have taken the same test.

The tests that follow in Chapters 1, 2 and 3 are divided into three main sections: verbal aptitude, spatial aptitude and numerical aptitude.

Chapter 4 consists of four separate IQ tests, each consisting of a mixture of verbal questions, numerical questions and questions involving diagrammatic representation.

Note: Because they have been newly compiled for this book, the tests have not been standardized in comparison to scores obtained by other groups. Nevertheless there is a guide to assessing your performance at the end of each test and, because several of the tests relate to specific aptitudes, the results will give you the opportunity to identify your own particular strengths and weaknesses.

CHAPTER 1

Verbal aptitude

The definition of 'verbal aptitude' is the capacity for general lexical skills — the understanding of words and the ability to use them effectively.

People who possess a high level of verbal skills often excel in fields such as writing (author, journalist, editor, critic), teaching (language, drama), the legal profession (judge, barrister, lawyer) and personnel work (advocate, human resources, counsellor) and as actors, psychologists, interpreters and interviewers.

Mastery of words is seen by many as having in one's possession the ability to produce order out of chaos. Because of this it is argued that command of vocabulary is an essential measure of intelligence, with the result that verbal tests are widely used in IQ testing.

Verbal reasoning tests are designed to measure basic verbal aptitude. Typically such tests include spelling, grammar, word meanings, completing sentences, synonyms (words that are the same or similar in meaning to each other) and antonyms (words that are opposite in meaning to each other).

The exercises that follow test basic verbal aptitude in a number of disciplines, including synonyms, antonyms, analogy, odd one out and verbal comprehension.

For each test a performance assessment is provided. The time limit that is specified for completing each test should not be exceeded; otherwise your score will be invalidated.

Test 1 General verbal aptitude test

This test is a miscellaneous selection of 30 questions designed to measure language use or comprehension, and your ability to adapt to different types of question.

You have 60 minutes in which to answer the 30 questions.

You should read the instructions to each question carefully before attempting it.

1   Which word in brackets is most similar in meaning to the word in capitals?

ERSTWHILE (fallacious, deviant, previous, honest, candid)

_____

2   Which word in brackets is most similar in meaning to the word in capitals?

PEDESTRIAN (plinth, ordinary, slow, erudite, rueful)

_____

3   Which word in brackets is most similar in meaning to the word in capitals?

TENABLE (believable, alluring, steadfast, delicate, speculative)

_____

4   Which two words are closest in meaning?

rubicund, recurrent, allied, frequent, routine, tolerable

_____

5   Which two words are closest in meaning?

strange, formless, hectic, irregular, pallid, angry

---

6   Which two words are closest in meaning?

conciliatory, propitious, inspired, fortunate, compatible, routine

---

7   Which word in brackets is most opposite in meaning to the word in capitals?

SOOTHE (augment, inflame, ignore, depress, execute)

---

8   Which word in brackets is most opposite in meaning to the word in capitals?

PROSCRIBE (demolish, stifle, change, unify, allow)

---

9   Which word in brackets is most opposite in meaning to the word in capitals?

GOAD (resolve, halt, dissuade, warn, retract)

---

10   Which two words are most opposite in meaning?

bright, exemplary, meteoric, fundamental, gradual, level

---

11   Which two words are most opposite in meaning?

superlative, traumatic, subversive, relaxing, crucial, uncommitted

---

12   Which two words are most opposite in meaning?

ancient, recant, evoke, maintain, dissent, stand

---

13   Which two words are most opposite in meaning?

susceptible, clandestine, extreme, credulous, banal, immune

---

14   Which is the odd one out?

inch, metre, litre, foot, kilometre

---

15   Which is the odd one out?

adieu, salutation, sayonara, farewell, ciao

---

16   Which is the odd one out?

appendix, prologue, supplement, addendum, postscript

---

17   Which is the odd one out?

immutable, eternal, transitory, imperishable, indelible

---

18   Which is the odd one out?

corporation, entrepreneur, business, firm, conglomerate

---

19   Which is the odd one out?

auburn, chestnut, walnut, carmine, hazel

---

20   Amplify is to augment as aggravate is to: elevate, maximize, exacerbate, inflate, proliferate

---

21   Identify two words (one from each set of brackets) that form a connection (analogy), thereby relating to the words in capitals in the same way.

FLORA (vegetation, life, animals)

FAUNA (animals, plants, flowers)

---

22   Identify two words (one from each set of brackets) that form a connection (analogy), thereby relating to the words in capitals in the same way.

APHELION (planet, furthest, distance)

PERIHELION (nearest, sun, orbit)

---

23   Identify two words (one from each set of brackets) that form a connection (analogy), thereby relating to the words in capitals in the same way.

SQUARE (polygon, rectangle, rhombus)

CIRCLE (sphere, diameter, ellipse)

---

24   Identify two words (one from each set of brackets) that form a connection (analogy), thereby relating to the words in capitals in the same way.

SPRING (autumn, flower, bud)

SUMMER (tree, leaf, July)

---

25 Identical is to indistinguishable as comparable is to
(congruous, corresponding, analogous, homogeneous,
symmetry)

---

26 Which two words that sound alike, but are spelled differently,
mean:

require / to work or press into a mass

---

27 Which word means the same as the definitions on either side
of the brackets?

condition of extreme hardship (   ) to promise or pledge

---

28 What word can be placed in the brackets so that it forms
a word or phrase when tacked on to the end of the first word,
and another word or phrase when placed in front of the
second word?

double (   ) bar

---

29 Which 3 of the 10 three-letter bits can be combined to produce a word meaning deserving of respect or high regard?

ide, ima, ria, end, est, ent, ard, atu, ble, ile   *Credible*

ble .

---

30 Which 3 of the 10 three-letter bits can be combined to produce a word meaning an authoritative rule?

ina, tas, ord, ula, ate, ian, nce, cel, ion, pet

ate

Test 2 Word meanings test

This test measures your ability to distinguish between words that are frequently confused or misused in correspondence and conversation.

In each question you are provided with two definitions and two words. You must place each word alongside its correct definition.

You have 30 minutes in which to solve the 30 questions.

1 a type of coarse cloth _____

to solicit votes _____

canvas, canvass

2 noun: one who depends _____

adjective: depending on _____

dependent, dependant

3 in that place _____

belonging to them _____

their, there

4 impartial, unbiased _____

lacking interest _____

disinterested, uninterested

5 unbroken, connected _____

frequent, repeated _____

continual, continuous

6 verb: to give an opinion _____

noun: opinion given _____

advice, advise

7   how much? _____

how many? _____

amount, number

8   verb: to predict _____

noun: prediction _____

prophecy, prophesy

9   very small or unimportant _____

careless _____

negligent, negligible

10   unwilling, reluctant _____

dislike intensely _____

loath, loathe

11   making less dark _____

discharge of electricity in atmosphere _____

lightening, lightning

12   spirit of fortitude or endurance _____

of good conduct _____

moral, morale

13   verb: to bring about; noun: result _____

verb: to act on, to influence _____

affect, effect

14   every two years _____

twice a year _____

bi-annual, biennial

15   notice or point out likenesses _____

notice or point out differences _____

compare, contrast

16   body of water or electricity _____

small berry _____

currant, current

17   to hint _____

to deduce or conclude _____

imply, infer

18   stated in detail _____

implied but not expressed _____

explicit, implicit

19   impending, close at hand _____

abiding in, inherent _____

immanent, imminent

20   staff employed _____

individual, private _____

personal, personnel

21   smaller in amount _____

smaller in number _____

less, fewer

22   to inform _____

to evaluate _____

appraise, apprise

23 that which completes _____

commendation, praise _____

complement, compliment

24 faulty, incomplete _____

falling short _____

defective, deficient

25 to turn aside, divert _____

to take away from _____

detract, distract

26 more than ordinary _____

for a special occasion _____

especially, specially

27 naïve, innocent _____

cleverly contrived _____

ingenious, ingenuous

28 related to a judge, impartial _____

sensible, prudent _____

judicial, judicious

29 examples _____

priority _____

precedence, precedents

30 work with another _____

confirm, support a statement _____

corroborate, collaborate

Test 3 Grammar and comprehension

This test is a miscellaneous selection of 15 questions designed to measure language use or comprehension, and your ability to adapt to different types of question, including several involving the use of grammar and punctuation.

You have 90 minutes in which to complete the 15 questions.

1 As a craftsman he was extremely .... at creating artistic designs of metalwork and he was able to .... his son's suggestion to .... several of these creations, which enables them to be put to better use.

Insert the three words below into their correct positions in the above sentence.

adopt, adapt, adept

2 The .... had a .... to remain .... as the train left the platform.

Which is the only one of the following combinations that contains the correct three words to be inserted into the above sentence?

A. superintendant, tendency, stationary

B. superintendent, tendancy, stationary

C. superintendant, tendency, stationery

D. superintendent, tendency, stationary

E. superintendent, tendency, stationery

F. superintendant, tendancy, stationery

Answer | A |

3 Which one of the following sentences is grammatically correct?

   A. Although it's true that the football team's fame has spread far and wide, it's performance has been a great disappointment to the manager throughout the current season.

   B. Although it's true that the football team's fame has spread far and wide, its performance has been a great disappointment to the manager throughout the current season.

   C. Although it's true that the football teams' fame has spread far and wide, its performance has been a great disappointment to the manager throughout the current season.

   D. Although its true that the football teams' fame has spread far and wide, it's performance has been a great disappointment to the manager throughout the current season.

   E. Although it's true that the football teams' fame has spread far and wide, it's performance has been a great disappointment to the manager throughout the current season.

Answer [ ]

4 Which one of the following sentences is grammatically correct?

   A. 'Whose that young child?' exclaimed the lady, whose plants the child had just trampled down.

   B. 'Who's that young child?' exclaimed the lady, whose plants the child had just trampled down.

   C. 'Who's that young child?' exclaimed the lady, who's plants the child had just trampled down.

   D. 'Whose that young child?' exclaimed the lady, who's plants the child had just trampled down.

Answer [ ]

5 'I agree in .... that it is .... acceptable for pupils to remove their jackets during classes in very hot weather', said the school ...., 'but they must remain .... at all times.'

In which one of the following do the four words appear in the correct order in which they should be inserted into the above sentence?

A. principal, quite, principle, quiet

B. principle, quite, principal, quiet

C. principal, quiet, principle, quite

D. principle, quiet, principal, quite

Answer [   ]

6   Which one of the following sentences is grammatically correct?

A. The sisters'-in-law of the bride's cousins made their way into the church.

B. The sisters-in-law of the bride's cousins made there way into the church.

C. The sister's-in-law of the bride's cousins made there way into the church.

D. The sisters-in-law of the bride's cousins made their way into the church.

E. The sisters-in-law of the brides' cousins made their way into the church.

F. The sister's-in-law of the bride's cousins made their way into the church.

Answer [   ]

7   Quite a .... of .... can give .... to other ...., but in .... that .... is not very ...., ... rather as a .... than as a ....

Insert the 12 words below into their correct position in the above sentence.

shocks   most   serving   animals   fish   warning
highly   number   weapon   electric   capacity
developed

8   Most roots, from branching trees to tiny plants, have large herbs.

Change the position of five words only in the above sentence so that it then makes complete sense.

_____

_____

9   For .... of .... have tried to find .... in .... the .... of ....

Insert the 10 words below into their correct position in the above sentence.

famous   hidden   people   compilers   names
hundreds   anagram   meanings   rearranging   years

10   One of the .... with the use of .... is that they are .... only .... by the .... who has .... them and are, thus, not a .... of ....

Insert the 10 words below into their correct position in the above sentence.

very   understood   communication   often   used
means   problems   abbreviations   effective   person

11   Good stone ability is an excellent career success to banking jobs in accounting such as stepping or mathematical.

Change the position of just eight words in the above passage so that it makes complete sense.

_____

_____

12   It is .... to have, or .... , the .... to take what at .... glance may .... a .... and, after .... the .... , ... at a ....

Insert the 12 words below into their correct position in the above sentence.

arrive   ability   seem   extremely   first   problem
complications   satisfying   difficult   solution
unravelling   develop

13   Mathematical exercises are necessary puzzles in logic and no Sudoku knowledge is purely in order to solve them.

Change the position of just six words in the sentence above so that it makes complete sense.

_____

_____

14   Words are directly used to relevant topic that are not enclose generally to the main sentence of the brackets.

Change the position of just eight words in the sentence above so that it makes complete sense.

_____

_____

15   The ...., when ...., ... from its .... a .... which .... into .... when it .... in .... with the ....

Insert the 12 words below into their correct position in the above sentence.

comes   volatile   bombardier   turns   contact
posterior   fluid   gas   attacked   air   beetle   emits

Test 4 Advanced verbal aptitude test

This test is a selection of 30 miscellaneous verbal questions designed to measure language use or comprehension, your problem-solving capabilities and your ability to adapt to different types of question.

You have 120 minutes in which to solve the 30 questions.

You should read the instructions to each question carefully before you attempt it.

1   What is wormwood?

A. an oil- and vinegar-based salad dressing

B. a type of plant

C. a mixture from which paper is manufactured

D. rotten timber

E. tar-based liquid

Answer [   ]

2   What is plenitude?

A. absolute power

B. difficulty or distress

C. commonplace

D. abundance

E. a stable period of economic activity

Answer [   ]

3   DID TRUCE is an anagram of two 'this and that' words, CUT, DRIED (cut and dried). FIRST LOOPS is an anagram of which two other 'this and that' words?

_____

4   DID TRUCE is an anagram of two 'this and that' words, CUT, DRIED (cut and dried). TRAPS SISTERS is an anagram of which two other 'this and that' words?

_____

5

S		A
E	E	C
I	U	

Start at one of the four corner letters and spiral clockwise round the perimeter, finishing at the centre letter to spell out a nine-letter word. You must provide the missing letters.

6

N		T
U	E	
	T	A

Start at one of the four corner letters and spiral clockwise round the perimeter, finishing at the centre letter to spell out a nine-letter word. You must provide the missing letters.

7   Which one of the following is not an anagram of a country?
A THIN LAD
ALAS I MAY
OIL A COMB
A NOBLE CAR
BAG HANDLES

_____

8

N		T
U	E	
	T	A

Work from letter to letter horizontally and vertically, but not diagonally, to spell out a 12-letter word. You must find the starting point and provide the missing letters.

9

S		O	O
E	U	O	T
L		R	

Work from letter to letter horizontally and vertically, but not diagonally, to spell out a 12-letter word. You must find the starting point and provide the missing letters.

10 Change one letter only in each of the words below to produce a familiar phrase.

COLD AS DAY

_____

11 Change one letter only in each of the words below to produce a familiar phrase.

NO TOP CAR

_____

12   A familiar phrase has had the initial letters of each word and its word boundaries removed. What is the phrase?

ITNHEENCE

_____

13   CENTIMETRE POLE is an anagram of which two words that are similar in meaning?

Clue: unabridged

_____

14

Read clockwise round each circle to find two words that are opposite in meaning. You must find the starting points and provide the missing letters.

_____

15   Only one group of five letters below can be rearranged to spell out a five-letter word in the English language. Identify the word.

GTOPA

DICOL

HWTCA

ACULT

TPRON

_____

16   Combine six of the three-letter bits to produce two words that are synonyms.

son   ent   ify   res   tor   cre   per   ely   rep   mis

_____

17   I am moving the part of my anatomy that contains the chief ganglia of the nervous system causing it to come into contact with a structure erected from rectangular blocks. What am I doing?

_____

18   The clue LACONIC HEALTH PROFESSIONAL leads to which pair of rhyming words?

_____

19   Solve the clues below. The letters XYZ in each word are the same three letters, which is a familiar three-letter word.

X Y Z * * *   a cogwheel with a small number of teeth

* X Y Z * *   pertaining to the backbone

* * X Y Z *   lying on the back

* * * X Y Z   a seedling apple

_____

20

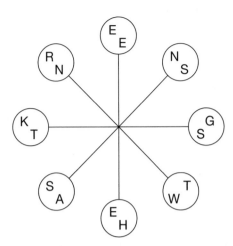

Work clockwise to spell out two eight-letter words that are antonyms. The letters in each word are consecutive, all letters are used once each and each word starts in a different circle. Each word takes one letter only from each circle.

21

E	S	H		
E	D	A		
A	P	R	R	F
		T	O	O
		N	F	E

Each nine-letter square contains the letters of a word. Find the two nine-letter words that are synonyms.

---

22 HAIL NOT THE HOUR is an anagram of what phrase (6–4–4 letters long) that means sanctimonious?

_____

23 ERRANT OR LOOSE is an anagram of what phrase (6–2–5 letters long) that means eventually?

_____

24 AGE ABLE PORT

Which is the only word below that shares a certain feature with the three words above?

OPEN WORD TALE END CAN

_____

25 Combine 4 of the 10 bits below to produce a word meaning spy.

con   per   esd   ess   eav   ric   erc   ome   rop   ant

_____

26

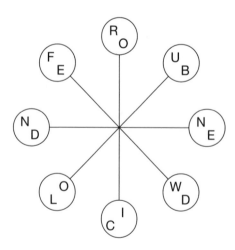

Work clockwise to spell out 2 eight-letter words that are synonyms. The letters in each word are consecutive, all letters are used once each and each word starts in a different circle. Each word takes one letter only from each circle.

_____

27

H	M	T	A	N	R	H	P	T	H
U	A	E	I	I	I	U	E	O	A
*	*	*	*	*	*	*	*	*	*

Insert a phrase (2–3–5 letters long), meaning definitely or certainly, on the bottom line to complete 10 three-letter words reading downwards.

_____

28

N	E	U		
R	E	A		
X	B	T	E	E
		D	L	I
		G	D	H

Each nine-letter square contains the letters of a word. Find the two nine-letter words that are synonyms.

_____

29

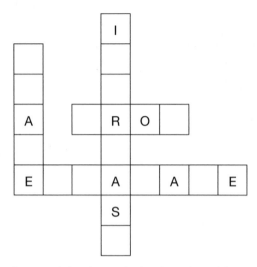

Insert the remaining letters below into the grid to produce four interlinked words, three synonyms and an antonym.

ASNG

BTCC

WLTEE

30 Which letter can be added to a word meaning BLEMISH to produce a word meaning OVERBURDEN?

R   T   D   M

———————————————————————

CHAPTER 2

Spatial aptitude

The definition of 'spatial' is pertaining to space, and spatial abilities mean the perceptual and cognitive abilities that enable a person to deal with spatial relations.

The questions within such tests typically take the form of a series of shapes or diagrams from which you have to pick the odd one out, identify which should come next in a sequence from a set of alternatives, choose from a set of alternatives the diagram that will complete an analogy or find the missing element in a matrix of figures. The ability being investigated in this type of test is how well a person is able to identify patterns and meaning from what might appear at first glance random or very complex information.

Such tests are referred to as culture-free or culture-fair, and are designed to be free from any cultural bias, so that no advantage is derived by individuals of one culture relative to those of another. In other words, they eliminate language factors or other skills that might be closely tied to one particular culture.

People who possess a high level of spatial aptitude often excel in fields such as architecture, photography, engineering design and decorating, and as artists, carpenters, landscape designers, cartoon animators, guides, fashion designers, shop fitters and civil engineers.

The tests in this chapter are all culture-fair and rely totally on diagrammatical representation. As well as testing your ability to deal with problems in a structured and analytical way, many are also designed to make you think laterally and creatively.

Test 1 General spatial aptitude test

Test one consists of 20 questions that will test your general spatial appreciation. As there are several different types of questions within the test, it is necessary to read the instructions to each question before attempting it.

You have 90 minutes in which to attempt the 20 questions.

1   Which is the odd one out?

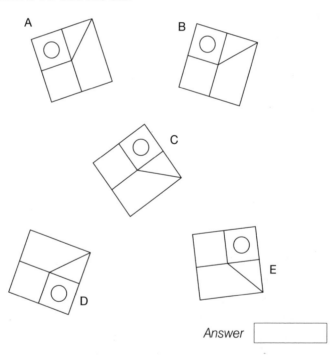

Answer [   ]

2

Which is the missing circle?

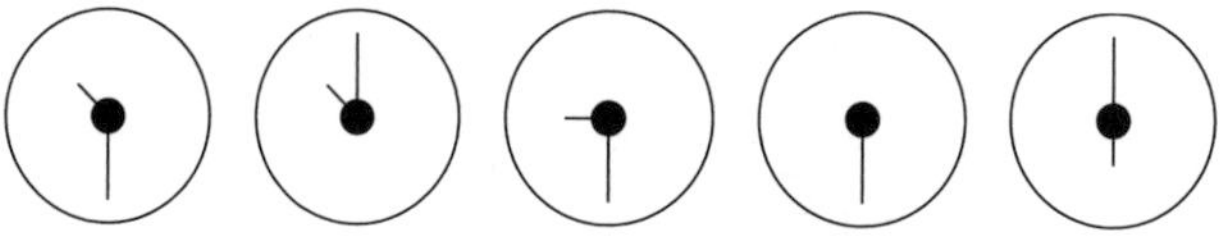

Answer _____

3

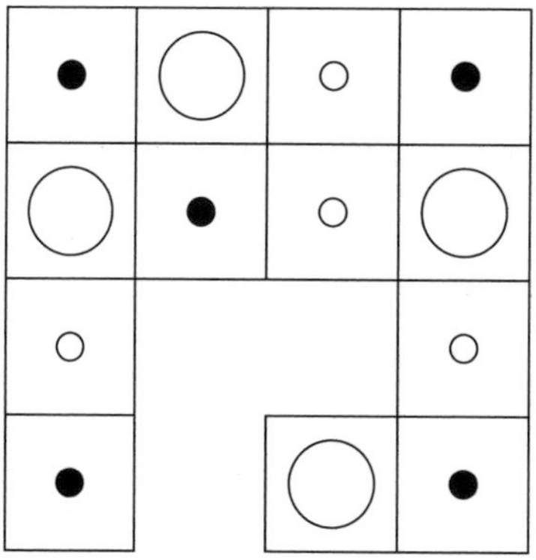

Which is the missing section?

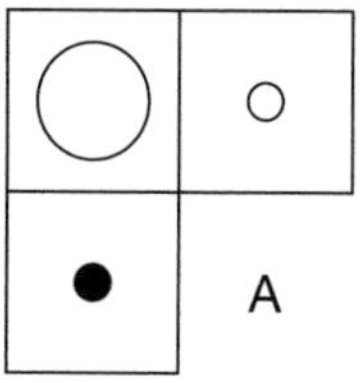

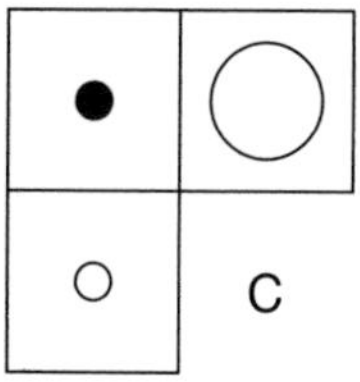

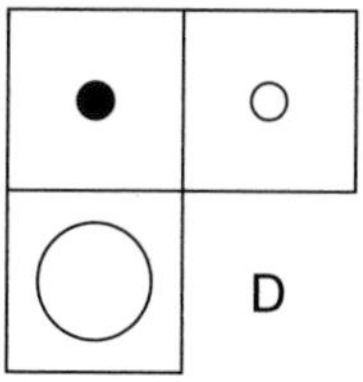

Answer _____

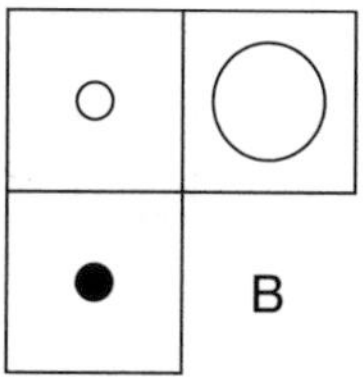

4

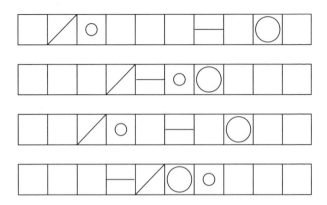

What comes next in the above sequence?

A

B

C

D

E

Answer

5   Which is the odd one out?

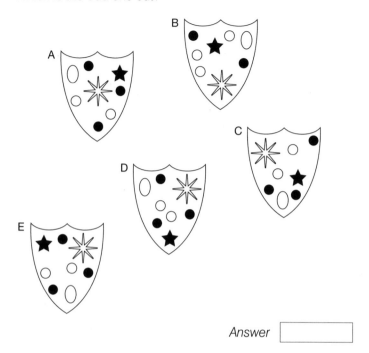

Answer [   ]

6

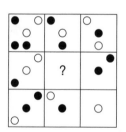

Which is the missing tile?

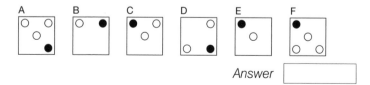

Answer [   ]

7   Which is the odd one out?

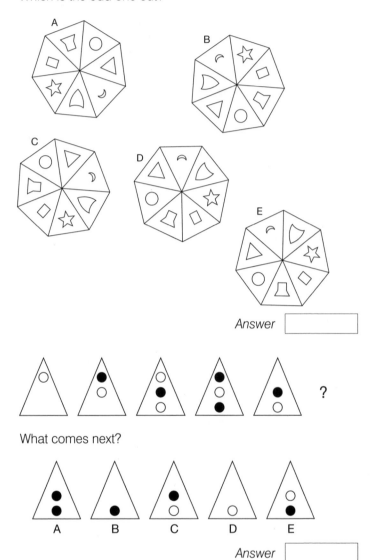

Answer [   ]

8

What comes next?

A   B   C   D   E

Answer [   ]

9   Which is the odd one out?

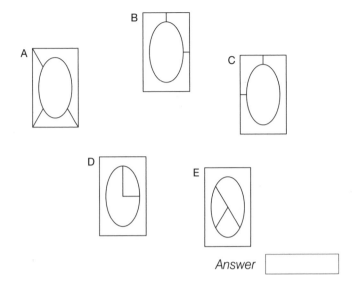

Answer [   ]

10   Which is the odd one out?

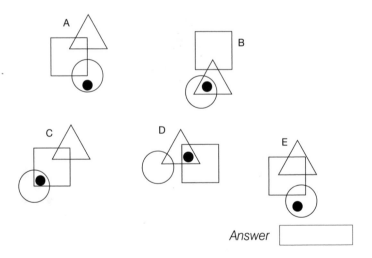

Answer [   ]

11

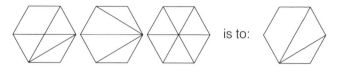

is to:

as:

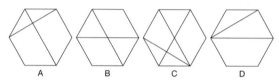

is to:

A   B   C   D

Answer [   ]

12

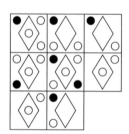

Which is the missing tile?

A   B   C   D   E   F

Answer [   ]

13

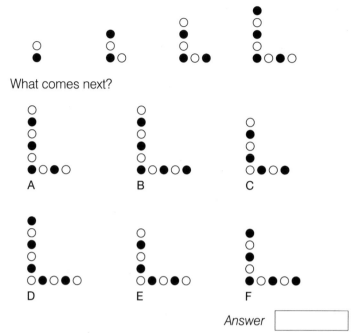

What comes next?

Answer [   ]

14

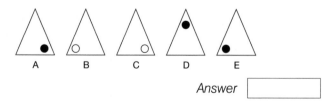

Which triangle should replace the one with the question mark?

Answer [   ]

15   Which is the odd one out?

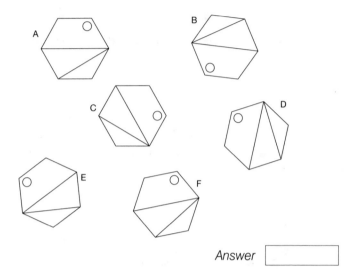

Answer [   ]

16

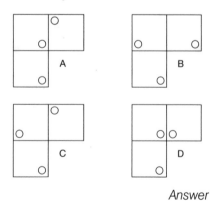

Which is the missing section?

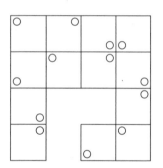

Answer [   ]

17

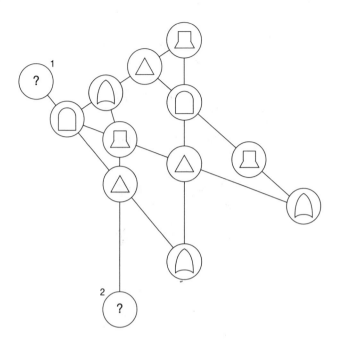

Which two symbols should replace the question marks?

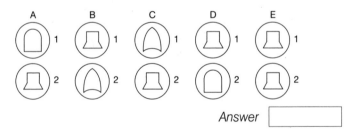

Answer

18   Which is the odd one out?

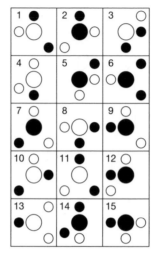

Answer [   ]

19

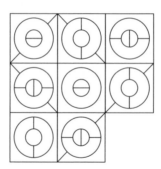

Which is the missing tile?

A   B   C

D   E   F

Answer [   ]

20

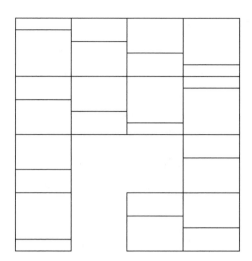

Which is the missing section?

A

B

C

D

Answer

Test 2 Logical analysis test

A definition of 'logical' is analytic or deductive, and this description can be applied to someone who is capable of reasoning or using reason in an orderly, cogent fashion.

The questions in this test can all be solved using logical analysis. In each question you are given three equations. In each of these the contents of the first two boxes determine the contents of the third box. One of the equations is incomplete and by using the same logic as for the two complete ones you must work out which is the correct box from the five options provided.

Before commencing the test it is recommended that you study the two examples provided.

Example 1

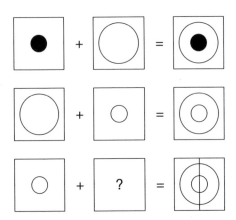

Which is the missing square?

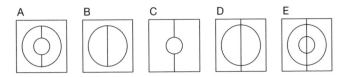

Answer: D

Explanation: The contents of box 1 added to the contents of box 2 equal the contents of box 3.

Example 2

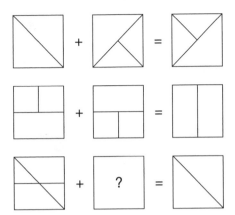

Which is the missing square?

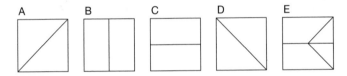

Answer: C

Explanation: The contents of box 1 added to the contents of box 2 equal the contents of box 3. However, when two lines appear in the same position in the first two boxes they do not then appear in box 3. In other words they are cancelled out.

You now have 60 minutes in which to complete the following 10 questions.

1

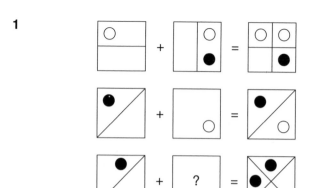

Which is the missing square?

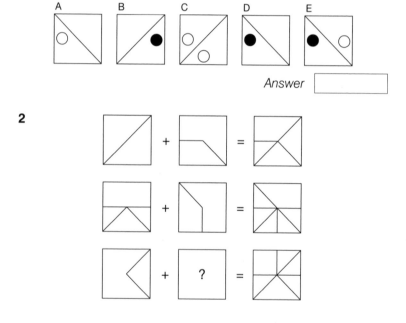

Answer [   ]

2

Which is the missing square?

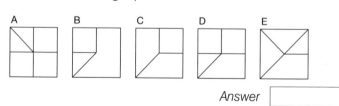

Answer [   ]

3

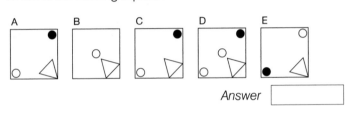

Which is the missing square?

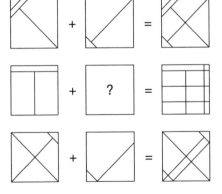

Answer [   ]

4

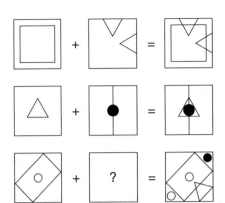

Which is the missing square?

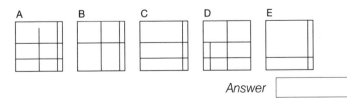

Answer [   ]

5

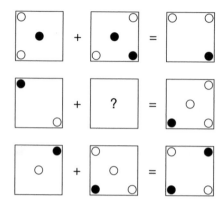

Which is the missing square?

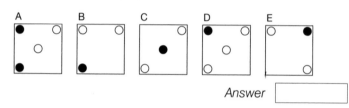

Answer

6

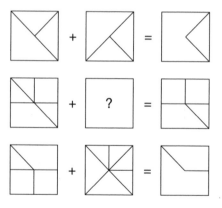

Which is the missing square?

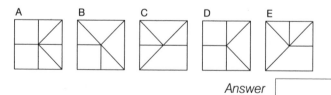

Answer

7

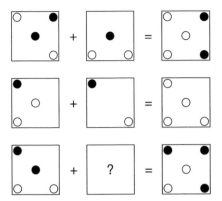

Which is the missing square?

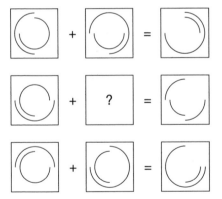

Answer [   ]

8

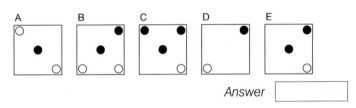

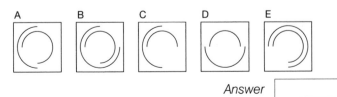

Which is the missing square?

Answer [   ]

9

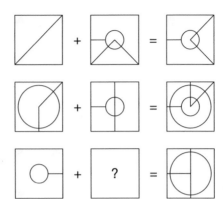

Which is the missing square?

A   B   C   D   E

Answer

10

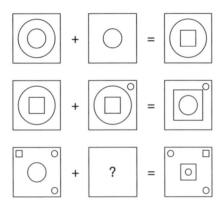

Which is the missing square?

A   B   C   D   E

Answer

Test 3 Advanced matrix test

The 10 questions here are designed to test and exercise your appreciation of pattern and design, your ability to think logically and your ability to concentrate and work quickly and analytically under pressure.

In each array of tiles, looking at lines across and down, the first two tiles are combined to produce the third tile, with the exception that like symbols are cancelled out. However, in each array one of the tiles is incorrect and should be replaced with one of the tiles A, B, C, D or E, in order to make the array correct looking both across each row and down each column.

In each question you are required to identify the tile that is incorrect and choose with which of the options, A, B, C, D or E, it should be replaced.

You have 90 minutes in which to solve the 10 questions.

1

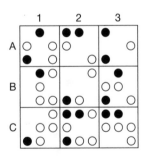

Looking at lines across and down, if the first two tiles are combined to produce the third tile, with the exception that like symbols are cancelled out, which of the above tiles is incorrect, and with which of the tiles below should it be replaced?

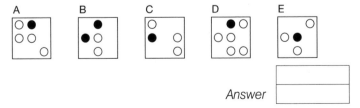

Answer

2

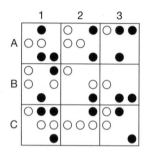

Looking at lines across and down, if the first two tiles are combined to produce the third tile, with the exception that like symbols are cancelled out, which of the above tiles is incorrect, and with which of the tiles below should it be replaced?

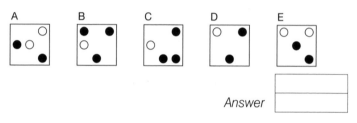

Answer

3

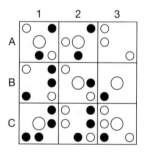

Looking at lines across and down, if the first two tiles are combined to produce the third tile, with the exception that like symbols are cancelled out, which of the above tiles is incorrect, and with which of the tiles below should it be replaced?

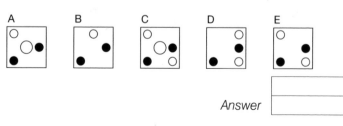

Answer

4

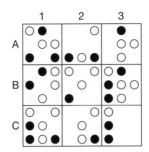

Looking at lines across and down, if the first two tiles are combined to produce the third tile, with the exception that like symbols are cancelled out, which of the above tiles is incorrect, and with which of the tiles below should it be replaced?

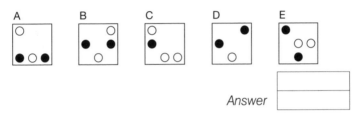

Answer

5

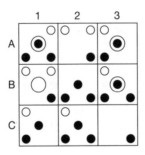

Looking at lines across and down, if the first two tiles are combined to produce the third tile, with the exception that like symbols are cancelled out, which of the above tiles is incorrect, and with which of the tiles below should it be replaced?

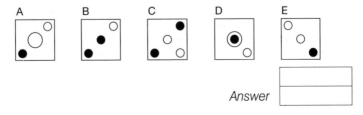

Answer

6

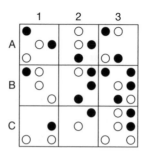

Looking at lines across and down, if the first two tiles are combined to produce the third tile, with the exception that like symbols are cancelled out, which of the above tiles is incorrect, and with which of the tiles below should it be replaced?

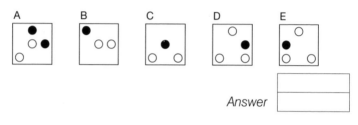

Answer

7

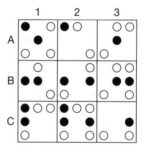

Looking at lines across and down, if the first two tiles are combined to produce the third tile, with the exception that like symbols are cancelled out, which of the above tiles is incorrect, and with which of the tiles below should it be replaced?

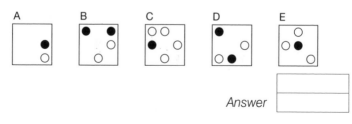

Answer

8

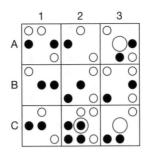

Looking at lines across and down, if the first two tiles are combined to produce the third tile, with the exception that like symbols are cancelled out, which of the above tiles is incorrect, and with which of the tiles below should it be replaced?

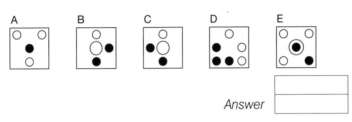

Answer

9

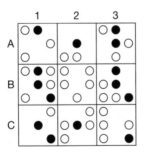

Looking at lines across and down, if the first two tiles are combined to produce the third tile, with the exception that like symbols are cancelled out, which of the above tiles is incorrect, and with which of the tiles below should it be replaced?

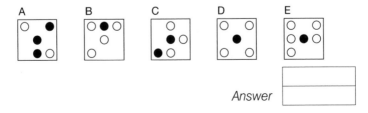

Answer

10

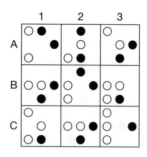

Looking at lines across and down, if the first two tiles are combined to produce the third tile, with the exception that like symbols are cancelled out, which of the above tiles is incorrect, and with which of the tiles below should it be replaced?

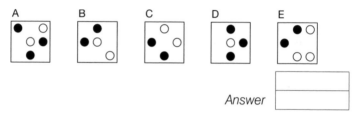

Answer

CHAPTER 3

Numerical aptitude

We all require some numerical skills in our lives, whether it is to calculate our weekly shopping bill or to budget how to use our monthly income. Mathematical intelligence tests generally explore your ability to reason and to perform basic arithmetic functions.

Numerical (mathematical) intelligence is a strong indicator of general intelligence, as many everyday tasks require arithmetical operations or thought processes even though numbers may not be involved.

Numerical questions are widely used in IQ testing and, as numbers are international, numerical tests are regarded as being culture-fair, or culture-free, and designed to be free from any particular cultural bias so that no advantage is derived by individuals of one culture relative to those of another.

Tests of numerical aptitude are frequently designed to test powers of logic and ability to deal with problems in a structured and analytical way. Such tests enable employers to test the numerical aptitude of candidates and to determine their proficiency and the extent of their knowledge when dealing with numbers, and their ability to apply this knowledge to the solving of mathematical problems.

Good mathematical ability is an excellent stepping stone to career success in jobs such as accounting or banking.

People who possess a high level of numerical skills also often excel in jobs such as auditor, business consultant, financial analyst, mathematics or science teacher, quantity surveyor, tax adviser, company secretary, computer programmer or stockbroker.

Test 1 Mental arithmetic

The following is a mental arithmetic speed test of 30 questions, which gradually increase in difficulty as the test progresses.

You should work quickly and calmly and try to think at all times of the quickest and most efficient way of tackling the questions.

The use of a calculator is not permitted in this test, and only the answer should be committed to paper, the object of the test being that all the working out is done in your head.

You have 45 minutes in which to solve the 30 questions.

1   What is 9 multiplied by 8?

Answer

2   What is 267 divided by 3?

Answer

3   What is 19 multiplied by 11?

Answer

4   What is 80% of 160?

Answer

5   Multiply 12 by 6 and divide by 3

Answer

6   Divide 42 by 7 and add 13

Answer

7   What is 60% of 250?

Answer

8   What is 5/6 of 360?

Answer

9   Multiply 18 by 12 and subtract 17

Answer

10   What is 9/8 of 200?

Answer

11   What is 20% of 135 plus 35?

Answer

12   Multiply 5 by 8 by 3

Answer

13   Divide 28 by 7 and add it to 15 multiplied by 5

Answer

14   What is 595 divided by 7?

Answer

15   Add 28 + 27 + 39 + 18 + 36

Answer

16   What is 35% of 150?

Answer

17   What is 45 multiplied by 19?

Answer

18   What is 3/8 of 128?

Answer

19   What is 1257 less 749?

Answer

20   Divide 126 by 14

Answer

21   What is 45% of 120?

Answer

22   Subtract 869 from 2482

Answer

23   Multiply 72 by 19

Answer

24   What is 1000 divided by 16?

Answer

25   Add 3/4 of 216 to 3/5 of 75

Answer

26   Add 963 to 471

Answer

27   Multiply 49 by 11

Answer

28   What is 12/16 expressed as a decimal?

Answer

29   Deduct 4/7 of 49 from 100

Answer [　　　　　　]

30   Divide 2682 by 894

Answer [　　　　　　]

Test 2 Numerical sequence test

In a numerical sequence test it is necessary to identify a pattern that is occurring in the sequence.

The numbers in the sequence may be progressing, or they may be decreasing. In some cases they may be both progressing and decreasing within the sequence, and in some cases two separate sequences may be interwoven. It is up to you to determine which of these is occurring and to continue the sequence by providing the missing number(s) indicated by the question mark(s) in each question.

The use of a calculator is not permitted in this test.

A time limit of 20 minutes is allowed in which to complete the 15 questions.

1   0, 1, 2, 3, 5, 7, 9, 12, 15, 18, ?

Answer [　　　　　　]

2   3, 6, 12, 21, 33, ?

Answer [　　　　　　]

3   1000, 975, 925, 850, 750, ?

Answer [　　　　　　]

4   1, 10, 2.5, 7.5, 4, 5, ?, ?

Answer [　　　　　　]

5   12,   8.5,   5,   1.5,   ?

Answer

6   8,   16,   64,   128,   512,   1024,   ?

Answer

7   12,   11,   9,   6,   2,   ?

Answer

8   1,   1.5,   3,   7.5,   21,   ?

Answer

9   2,   6,   9,   27,   30,   90,   93,   ?

Answer

10   5,   6,   7,   8,   10,   12,   14,   20,   ?,   ?

Answer

11   100,   99,   96,   91,   84,   75,   64,   ?

Answer

12   19,   38,   57,   76,   95,   114,   ?

Answer

13   2,   5,   12,   27,   58,   121,   ?

Answer

14   10,   9.75,   9.25,   8.5,   7.5,   6.25,   ?

Answer

15   10,   11.75,   9.25,   11,   8.5,   ?

Answer

Test 3 Working with numbers

This test is a battery of 20 questions designed to measure your ability to work with numbers and think numerically.

A time limit of 120 minutes is allowed in which to complete the 20 questions. The use of a calculator is permitted in this test.

1

45	9	5	10	44
2	24	14	4	48
11	18	13	27	6
15	3	15	1	27
12	8	7	36	16

Looking at straight lines horizontally, vertically or diagonally, what number is three places away from itself multiplied by 3, two places away from itself less 3, three places away from itself divided by 2 and two places away from itself less 1?

Answer [ ]

2 Find five consecutive numbers in the list below that total 21.

5823639472165834259423

Answer [ ]

3

1	3	6	8	11
4	6		11	14
6		11	13	16
9	11		16	19
11	13	16		21

Which is the missing section?

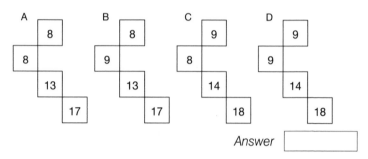

Answer [   ]

4   9 2 6 5 9 2 1 7 5 3 8 9 4 1 6 8 9 7 2 4 8 3

Add together all the even numbers in the above list that are immediately followed by an odd number.

Answer [   ]

5   3 2 9 7 4 8 5 7 9 2 4 5 7 1 9 3 8 4 1 8 2 5

What is the mean of all the numbers greater than 6 in the list above?

Answer [   ]

6   Insert the numbers listed into the circles so that — for any
particular circle — the sum of the numbers in the circles connected to it equals the value corresponding to that circled
number in the list. For example:

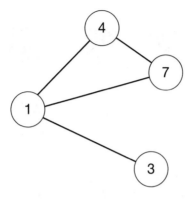

1 = 14 (4 + 7 + 3)
3 = 1
4 = 8 (1 + 7)
7 = 5 (1 + 4)

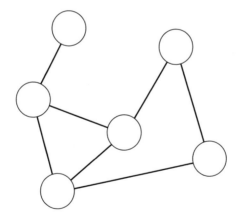

1 = 13
2 = 4
3 = 8
4 = 5
5 = 11
6 = 9

7   Insert numbers into the remaining blank squares so that the sums in each line and column are correct. All numbers to be inserted are less than 10.

	×		÷		=	4
+	■	−	■	+	■	+
	+		+	3	=	
−	■	−	■	÷	■	÷
	−	1	×		=	
=	■	=	■	=	■	=
2	+		÷		=	

8   If Phil gives Jill £20.00 the money they each have is in the ratio 1:3, but if Jill gives Phil £20.00 the money they each have is exactly the same. How much money have Phil and Jill each before they exchange any money?

Answer [   ]

9   What is 3/8 divided by 9/16 ?

Answer [   ]

10

3	2	5	4
1	0		
4		6	5
2	1	4	3

Which is the missing section?

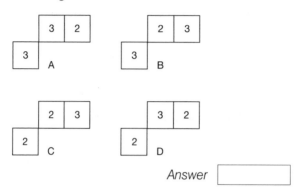

Answer [   ]

11 Multiply the second-highest odd number in the right-hand grid by the second-lowest even number in the left-hand grid.

15	28	13	12	20
29	42	34	58	48
84	64	11	18	27
89	16	36	25	26
17	72	41	61	40

49	11	29	22	61
16	63	47	14	51
53	57	18	37	21
55	19	84	72	59
35	14	81	13	96

Answer [   ]

12

5	29	7	34
12	16	4	9
20	8	2	11
3	13	6	18

14	12	17	?
8	2	7	3
22	4	19	10
15	6	1	16

Insert the missing number in the right-hand grid so that the 16 numbers in each grid then total the same.

Answer

13   Jo's age plus Mo's age is 27;

and Jo's age plus Flo's age is 38;

and Mo's age plus Flo's age is 33.

Therefore, how old are Jo, Mo and Flo?

Answer

14   983 : 75

294 : 22

763 : 45

579 : ?

Answer

15

2	7
8	6

2	?
7	3

Which number is missing from the right-hand grid so that when multiplied together the product of the four numbers in the left-hand grid is the same as the product of the four numbers in the right-hand grid?

Answer

16

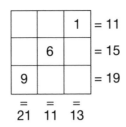

		1	= 11
	6		= 15
9			= 19

= = =
21 11 13

Insert the remaining numbers from 1 to 9 in the grid so that adding the numbers across and down gives the column and row numbers outside the grid.

17

D	B	D	C	31
D	C	B	A	24
A	C	D	C	23
B	B	B	C	23

29 22 32 ?

Each letter represents the same number (ranging between 3 and 10 inclusive). Seven of the resultant row and column totals are given. What is the missing total?

Answer [   ]

18

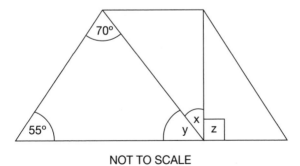

70°
55°
x
y z

NOT TO SCALE

What is the value of angle x?

Answer [   ]

19

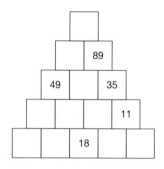

Each number is the sum of the two numbers immediately below it in the pyramid. Fill in all the missing numbers.

20 Harry has twice as many as Barry. Altogether they have 207. How many each have Harry and Barry?

Answer

Test 4 Numerical problem solving

The 15 questions in this test are designed to assess your aptitude at applying your basic mathematical knowledge in order to solve correctly each problem as quickly as possible, and your ability to deal with problems in a structured and analytical way.

The use of a calculator is permitted in this test.

You have 60 minutes in which to answer the 15 questions.

1 Which number is 63 less than 8 times itself?

Answer

2 A motorist knows four different routes from London to Oxford and three different routes from Oxford to Gloucester. How many different routes does the motorist know from London to Gloucester via Oxford?

Answer

3   My sister Suzie says that in two years she will be twice as old as she was four years ago. How old is my sister Suzie now?

Answer [   ]

4   Amy visits three stores. At the first store she spends half of her money plus £20.00, at the second store she spends half the money she has left plus £10.00 and at the third store she spends half of what she has left plus £20.00. She is now out of money. How much money did Amy start out with?

Answer [   ]

5   How many minutes is it before 12 noon if 32 minutes ago it was three times as many minutes past 9 am?

Answer [   ]

6   In four years' time the combined age of my three cousins and me will be 208. What will be the combined age in seven years' time?

Answer [   ]

7   Mo, Jo and Flo share out a certain sum of money between them. Mo receives 5/8, Jo receives 0.25 and Flo receives £7.50. How much is the original sum of money?

Answer [   ]

8   Mary has a budget of £180.00 to spend on her day out. She spends 5/9 of the £180.00 in the morning, 0.375 of the £180.00 in the afternoon and writes out a cheque for £45.00 in the evening at a restaurant. What is her financial situation at the end of the day?

Answer [   ]

9   How many boxes measuring 1 metre × 1 metre × 50 cm can be packed into a container measuring 8 × 6 × 6 metres?

Answer [   ]

10 A market trader received a consignment of eggs and to his dismay found that 175 were cracked, which was 14% of the total consignment. How many eggs were in the consignment?

Answer [   ]

11 The average of three numbers is 29. The average of two of these numbers is 41. What is the third number?

Answer [   ]

12 A train travelling at a speed of 80 mph enters a tunnel that is 2.5 miles long. The length of the train is 0.5 mile. How long does it take for all of the train to pass through the tunnel from the moment the front enters to the moment the rear emerges?

Answer [   ]

13 I travel to work by bus and train. If my bus journey takes 28 minutes and my train journey takes 35 minutes longer, what is the total travelling time in hours and minutes?

Answer [   ]

14 At the Friday morning market a grocer sold 720 items of fruit consisting of a mixture of grapefruit, oranges and pears in the ratio 3 : 4 : 2 respectively. How many of each fruit did the grocer sell?

Answer [   ]

15 Cartons of yoghurt cost 4 pence (£0.04) more if bought individually than if bought in packs of 6. If a pack of 6 costs £2.76, what is the cost of 5 cartons?

Answer [   ]

CHAPTER 4

IQ tests

An IQ (intelligence quotient) test is a standardized test designed to measure human intelligence as distinct from attainments.

Intelligence quotient is an age-related measure of intelligence level. The word 'quotient' means the result of dividing one quantity by another, and one definition of intelligence is mental ability or quickness of mind.

Usually, IQ tests consist of a graded series of tasks, each of which has been standardized with a large representative population of individuals in order to establish an average IQ of 100 for each test.

It is generally accepted that a person's mental age remains constant in development to about the age of 13, after which it is shown to slow up, and beyond the age of 18 little or no improvement is found.

When the IQ of a child is measured, the subject attempts an IQ test that has been standardized, with an average score recorded for each age group. Thus a 10-year-old child who scored the result that would be expected of a 12-year-old would have an IQ of 120, or 12/10 × 100.

Since little or no improvement is found after the age of 18, adults have to be judged on an IQ test whose average score is 100, and the results graded above and below this norm according to known test scores.

Like so many distributions found in nature, the distribution of IQ takes the form of a fairly regular bell curve, in which the average score is 100 and similar proportions occur both above and below this norm.

There are many different types of IQ tests. However, a typical test might consist of three sections, with each testing a different ability (usually verbal reasoning, numerical ability and diagrammatic, or spatial, reasoning). In order to give you the opportunity to practise all the types of questions that you are likely to encounter in actual IQ tests, the tests that have been specially compiled for this book are multi-disciplinary and include a mix of verbal, numerical and diagrammatic questions, as well as additional questions involving logical thought processes, together with a degree of lateral thinking.

While it is generally accepted that a person's IQ remains constant throughout their life, and that they are therefore unable to increase their actual IQ, it is possible to improve one's performance on IQ tests by practising the many different types of question and learning to recognize the recurring themes.

The four IQ tests that follow have been newly compiled for this book and are therefore not standardized, so an actual IQ assessment cannot be given. However, a guide to assessing your performance for each test is provided.

A time limit of 120 minutes is allowed for each test. The correct answers are given in Chapter 5 and you should award yourself 1 point for each completely correct answer. Calculators may be used to assist with solving numerical questions if preferred.

IQ test one

1   Which is the odd one out?

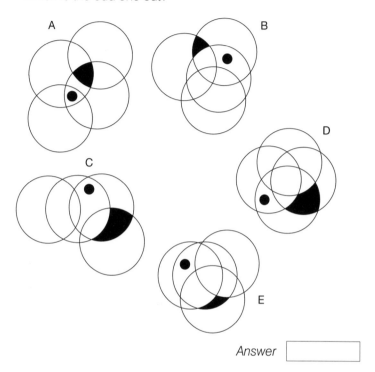

A   B   C   D   E

Answer [   ]

2   Which word in brackets is closest in meaning to the word in capitals?

SALUBRIOUS (healthy, practical, anaemic, arresting, sad)

_____

3   Place a word in the brackets that has the same meaning as the definitions either side of the brackets.

financial institution (   ) side of river

4   1, 1, 3, 3, 6, 7, 10, 13, 15, 21, ?, ?

Answer [   ]

5   The call centre received its highest number of enquiries between 3 pm and 4 pm, which was 60% more than the 600 enquiries it received between 2 pm and 3 pm. On average, how many enquiries per minute were received between 3 pm and 4 pm?

Answer

6

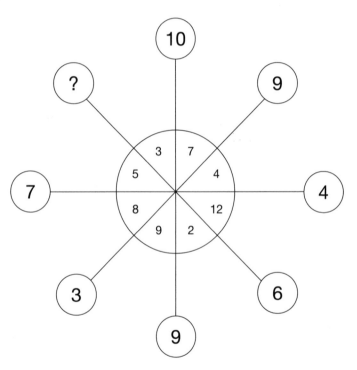

What number should replace the question mark?

Answer

7

4	3	5	4	6
2		3	2	4
3	2		3	5
1		2	1	3
2		3	2	4

Which is the missing section?

1	
	4
0	
1	

A

1	
	5
1	
0	

B

0	
	4
0	
1	

C

0	
	5
1	
0	

D

Answer [   ]

8   INEPT OLD BIRD is an anagram of which two words (4,8 letters long) that are similar in meaning?

Clue: courageous

Answer [   ]

9

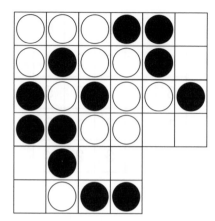

Which is the missing square?

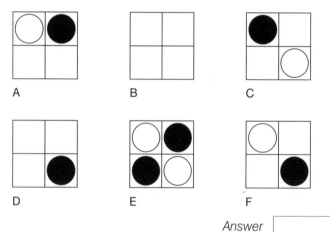

Answer [   ]

10

S	O	R	T
	T	A	S
	E	R	E

Work from letter to letter horizontally and vertically, but not diagonally, to spell out a 12-letter word. You must find the starting point and provide the missing letters.

Answer [   ]

11 Use each letter of the newspaper headline below once only to spell out the names of three types of fruit.

CHEAP PIRACY TERROR

---

12 What word can be placed in the brackets so that it forms another word or phrase when tacked on to the end of the first word, and another word or phrase when placed in front of the second word?

SAND ( ) WORK

13

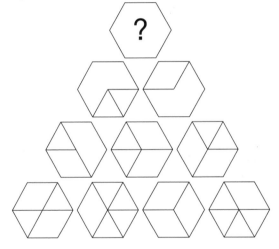

Which hexagon should replace the question mark?

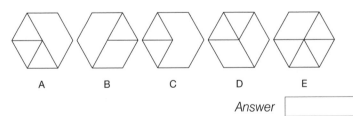

| A | B | C | D | E |

Answer

14 Which two words are most opposite in meaning?

unsavoury, tawdry, graceful, irksome, undemanding, potent

_____

15

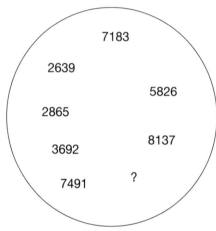

7183

2639

5826

2865

8137

3692

7491   ?

What number is missing?

Answer [ ]

16 What is the longest word in the English language that can be produced from the letters:

ARPDHLINEF

Answer [ ]

17

7	9	4	2
6	3	8	1
5	2	6	9
4	7	3	5

6	8		3
7	2	9	
	3	7	8
5	6	2	4

Fill in the three missing numbers.

18   Which of the following is not an anagram of an animal?

LEG ZEAL

GAUNT RONA

THE PANEL

BULL MARE

LOG RAIL

Answer

19

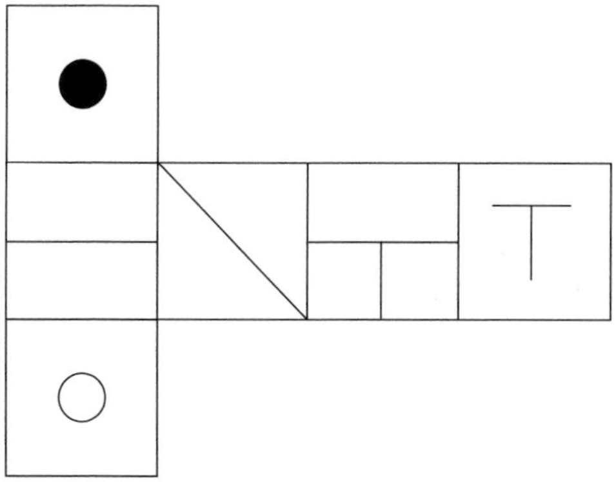

When the above is folded to form a cube, which is the only one of the following that *cannot* be produced?

Answer

20

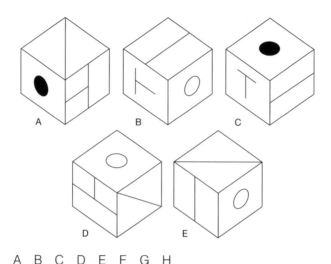

A B C D E F G H

What letter is two to the right of the letter which is four places to the left of the letter immediately to the right of the letter F ?

Answer

21

Which is the missing section?

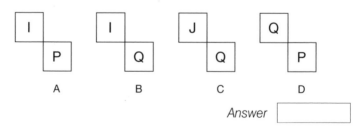

Answer

22   In four years' time Angela will be twice as old as Barry and four times as old as Carol. Three years ago Angela was three times as old as Barry. How old are Angela, Barry and Carol now?

23   Which is the odd one out?

mollify, congeal, muffle, macerate, assuage

24

is to:

as:

is to:

| A | B | C | D | E |

Answer [   ]

25   The third digit is two more than the first digit; the fourth digit is two more than the second digit; the second digit is five less than the third digit. Which two numbers below are being described?

3164, 4163, 6387, 1537, 6486, 5739, 2547, 7496, 3456, 5373

Answer [   ]

26   OLD, FIRM, OFFER, TOMATO

What word comes next, logically, in the above sequence?

verbal, quality, literal, candid, radiant

27

7	2	3	6
5	6	2	8
3	8	1	9
8	4	4	?

What number should replace the question mark?

Answer

28   What six-letter word can be placed in the brackets so that it forms another word or phrase when tacked on to the end of the first word, and another word or phrase when placed in front of the second word?

MAIN (   ) LINE

29   Identify two words (one from each set of brackets) that form a connection (analogy), thereby relating to the words in capitals in the same way.

DORMITORY (dine, teach, sleep)

REFECTORY (eat, store, cure)

30

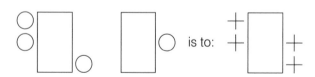

as:

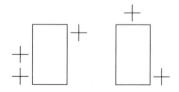

is to:

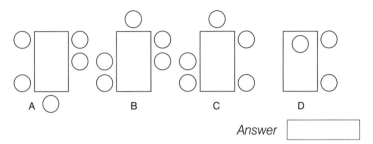

A   B   C   D

Answer [   ]

31   5 6 3 2 9 7 1 4 2 6 8 3 7 5 9 7 1

Delete all the numbers that appear more than once in the above list; then multiply the remaining numbers together. What is the answer?

_____

32   Place four of the nine three-letter bits together to produce a word meaning *histrionic*.

ama, alo, mel, iac, tic, ive, odr, geo, nal

_____

33   Which is the odd one out?

chord, tangent, hypotenuse, diameter, radius

_____

34   2, 7, 22, 67, 202, ?

What comes next?

Answer [   ]

35 How many lines appear below?

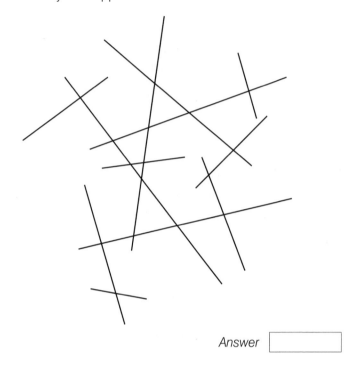

Answer

36 quadrangular is to square as annular is to:

clock, circle, year, cubic, figure

37 The ages of a group of people are:

34, 27, 36, 18, 15, 72, 67, 12, 24, 45

What percentage of people in the group are above the average age for the group?

Answer

38 Which two words that are spelled differently but have the same pronunciation mean:

summit / irritation

Answer

39

52	31	66	42
79	?	17	74
48	69	34	58
21	73	83	26

What number should replace the question mark?

Answer

40 Which four of the five pieces below can be fitted together to form a perfect square?

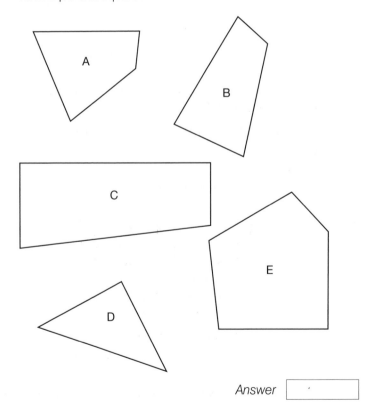

Answer

IQ test two

1

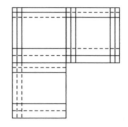

Which is the missing tile?

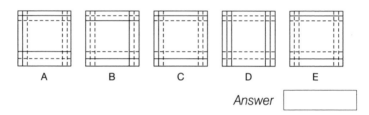

| A | B | C | D | E |

Answer [ ]

2 Solve the anagram in brackets (10-letter word) to complete a quotation by Sam Goldwyn.

I had a (NO MALT MENU) idea this morning, but I didn't like it.

_____

3

3	9	7	4	9	8
1	6	8	7	9	4
2	4	9	3	?	6

What number should replace the question mark?

Answer [ ]

4 velum is to palate as trachea is to: throat, windpipe, larynx, swallow, taste

Answer [ ]

5

1	4	7
4	3	9

3	7	5
7	5	5

4	?	6
6	8	2

What number should replace the question mark?

Answer [   ]

6 1864 is to 712

and 3925 is to 514

therefore 4859 is to ?

Answer [   ]

7

82	?	6

49	36	18

74	28	?

What numbers should replace the question marks?

The link between the three numbers on each line follows the same rule.

Answer [   ]

8 If meat in a river (3 in 6) is T(HAM)ES, can you find a metallic element in the surrounding conditions (4 in 11)?

_____

9

13	6	11
8	?	12
9	14	7

What number should replace the question mark?

Answer [   ]

10   Identify two words (one from each set of brackets) that form a connection (analogy), thereby relating to the words in capitals in the same way.

WAX (polish, lighten, increase)

WANE (distend, diminish, plummet)

_____

11   What word is missing from the brackets?

ileum (automobile) taboo

elite (   ) porch

12   Mal is one and a third times older than Sal and Sal is one and a third times older than Al. Together their combined ages total a magnificent 222 years. How old are Al, Sal and Mal?

_____

13   Place a word in the brackets that has the same meaning as the definitions either side of the brackets.

small piece of land (   ) conspiracy

14   How tall is a sapling that is 3 metres shorter than a fence that is four times higher than the sapling?

_____

15

Draw the missing tile from the above matrix.

16   386295

925683

863529

259368

?

What comes next?

Answer [   ]

17   Complete the words so that the two letters that end the first word start the second word and the two letters that end the second word start the third word, etc. The two letters that end the sixth word also start the first word, to complete the circle.

_ _ P I _ _

_ _ T T _ _

_ _ N G _ _

_ _ I R _ _

_ _ I G _ _

_ _ N U _ _

18

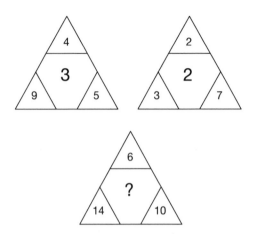

What number should replace the question mark?

Answer [   ]

19 Place a word in the brackets that has the same meaning as the definitions either side of the brackets.

abstain (   ) chorus of a song

20 Which word in brackets is closest in meaning to the word in capitals?

PHLEGMATIC (authentic, unemotional, alert, bourgeois, average)

21

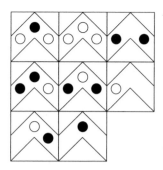

Which is the missing tile?

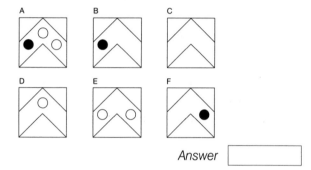

Answer

22 Which is the odd one out?

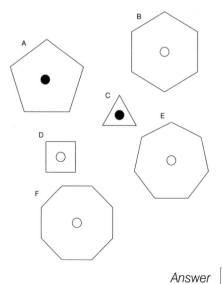

Answer

23   If F F the B represents the phrase Fortune Favours the Brave, what phrase is represented by H is the B P?

_____

24

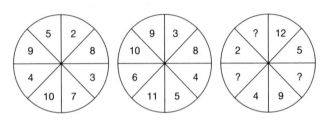

Which numbers should replace the question marks?

Answer [   ]

25   What word can be placed in the brackets so that it forms another word or phrase when tacked on to the end of the first word, and another word or phrase when placed in front of the second word?

home (   ) mark

26   Which word in brackets is most opposite in meaning to the word in capitals?

SUPPOSEDLY (never, blatant, undoubtedly, allegedly, rarely)

_____

27   1 ½, 4 ¼, ? , 9 ¾, 12 ½, 15 ¼

What number should replace the question mark?

Answer [   ]

28 Which three of the four pieces below can be fitted together to form a perfect circle?

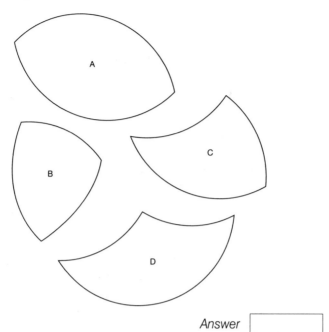

Answer [   ]

29

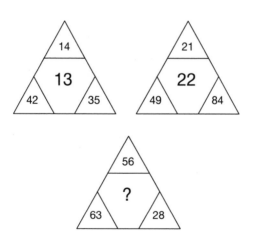

What number should replace the question mark?

Answer [   ]

30

A	B	C	D	E
F	G	H	I	J
K	L	M	N	O
P	Q	R	S	T
U	V	W	X	Y	Z

What letter is two below the letter immediately to the right of the letter that is three above the letter W?

Answer [   ]

31

T	U	
A		L
	I	T

Start at one of the four corner letters and spiral clockwise round the perimeter, finishing in the centre square, to spell out a nine-letter word. You must provide the missing letters.

32 Which is the odd one out?

maxim, fable, adage, epigram, proverb

33

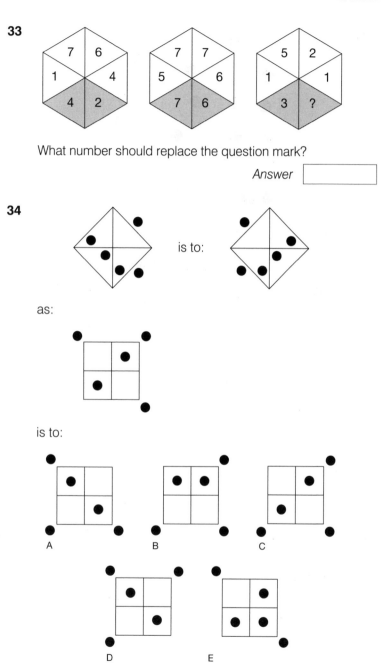

What number should replace the question mark?

Answer

34

is to:

as:

is to:

A

B

C

D

E

Answer

35

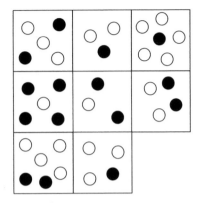

Which is the missing tile?

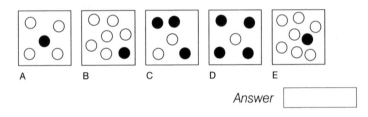

Answer [   ]

36   100, 93.5, 80.5, 61, 35, ?

What comes next?

Answer [   ]

37   What day and date comes 43 days after Saturday 24 June?

_____

38   A B C D E F G H

What letter is immediately to the right of the letter that comes midway between the letter two to the right of the letter A and the letter immediately to the left of the letter H?

Answer [   ]

39

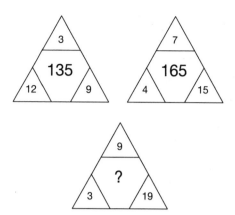

What number should replace the question mark?

Answer

40   contemplate is to meditate as contrive is to: project, devise, implement, draft, strategy

Answer

IQ test three

1

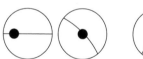 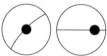

Which is the missing circle?

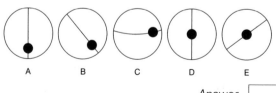

Answer

2   100, 1, 91.5, 9.5, 83, 18, 74.5, 26.5, ?, ?

What two numbers come next?

Answer

3 Identify two words (one from each set of brackets) that form a connection (analogy), thereby relating to the words in capitals in the same way.

URSINE (rabbit, sheep, bear)

VULPINE (fox, deer, wolf)

_____

4

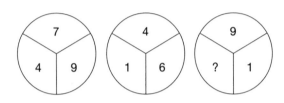

What number should replace the question mark?

Answer [   ]

5

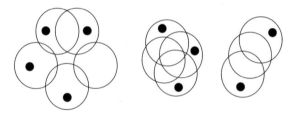

What comes next?

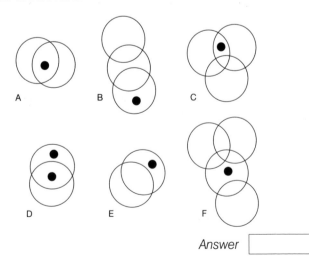

Answer [   ]

6

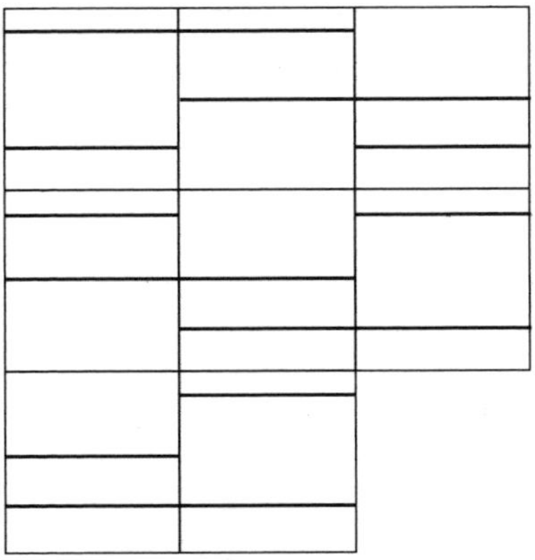

Which is the missing tile?

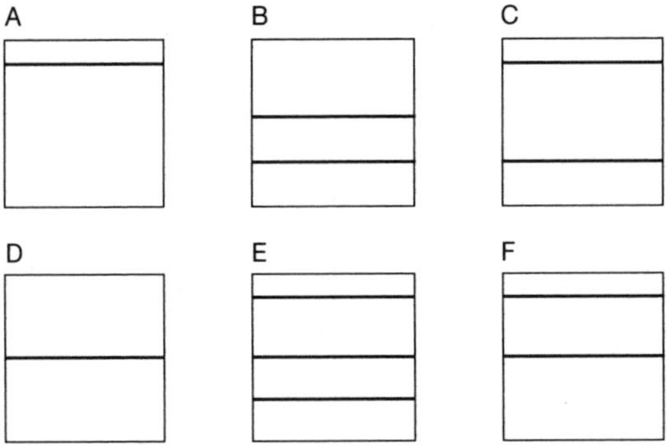

A B C

D E F

Answer [   ]

7   Only one group of five letters below can be rearranged to spell out a five-letter word in the English language. Identify the word.

KATOC

EFIMO

UNOPF

MEOPT

GULEP

Answer [   ]

8   Place a word in the brackets that has the same meaning as the definitions either side of the brackets.

A single instance or example of something (   ) receptacle

9

1	5	3	9
7	0	1	8
1	2	4	7
9	7	8	?

What two-digit number should replace the question mark?

Answer [   ]

10

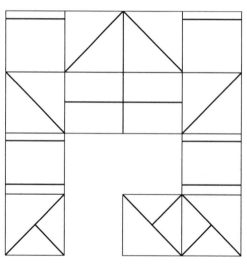

Which is the missing section?

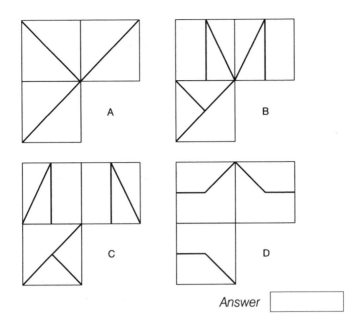

Answer [   ]

11 erg is to work as mach is to: engine, speed, power, force, pressure

Answer [   ]

12

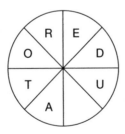

Insert the missing letter in order to spell out an eight-letter word reading clockwise.

13

O O O O O

Put the numbers 1 to 5 in the circles so that:

The sum of the numbers 2 and 1 and all the numbers between total 7.

The sum of the numbers 5 and 3 and all the numbers between total 15.

The sum of the numbers 4 and 3 and all the numbers between total 8.

The sum of the numbers 5 and 1 and all the numbers between total 12.

14   elegant   fearless   midshipman   elliptical   hackneyed

Which word below shares a common feature with the five words above?

relaxed, distribute, abdominal, goggles, simulate

15

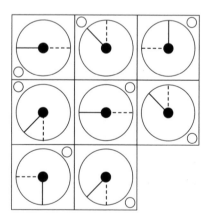

Which is the missing tile?

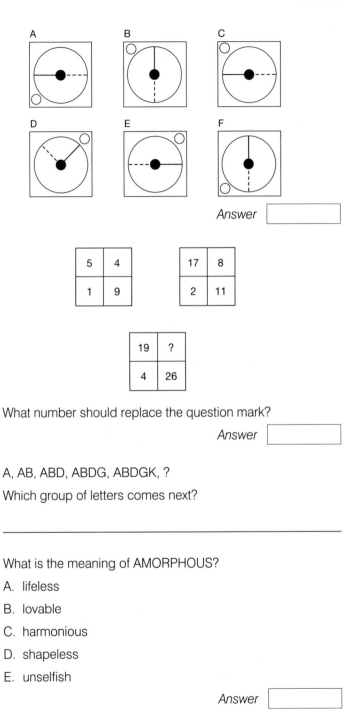

Answer [   ]

16

5	4
1	9

17	8
2	11

19	?
4	26

What number should replace the question mark?

Answer [   ]

17 A, AB, ABD, ABDG, ABDGK, ?

Which group of letters comes next?

_____

18 What is the meaning of AMORPHOUS?

A. lifeless

B. lovable

C. harmonious

D. shapeless

E. unselfish

Answer [   ]

19

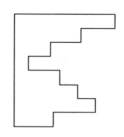

Which piece below can be fitted to the piece above to form a perfect square?

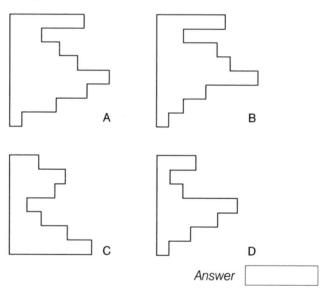

Answer [　　　　　]

20　7492836　　*　　89

　　　*　　　　　　*

　　638947　　　　798

　　　*　　　　　　*

　　74986　　*　　?

What number should replace the question mark?

Answer [　　　　　]

21 If my train journey takes 47 minutes and my taxi journey takes 19 minutes longer, what is my total travelling time in hours and minutes?

---

22 A familiar phrase has had its initial letters and word boundaries removed. What is the phrase?

SLAINSAY

---

23 What is the value of:

$$496 \times \left(\frac{384}{768} \right)^2$$

Answer [   ]

24

	T	
O	O	O
P	I	L

Start at one of the four corner squares and spiral clockwise round the perimeter to spell out a nine-letter word, finishing at the centre square. You must provide the missing letters.

25 In four years' time Sally will be twice as old as she was five years ago. How old is Sally now?

---

26   Which is the odd one out?

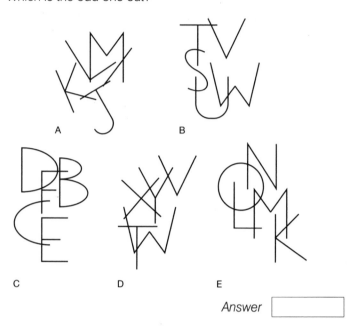

A   B

C   D   E

Answer [   ]

27   Change one letter only in each of the words below to produce a familiar phrase.

ON DEAL LINE

28

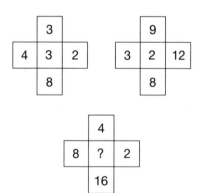

What number should replace the question mark?

Answer [   ]

29 Which word in brackets is most opposite in meaning to the word in capitals?

DEPRAVED (elated, cherished, chaste, lascivious, favoured)

30

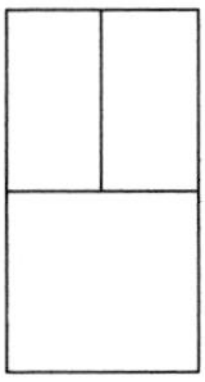

is to:

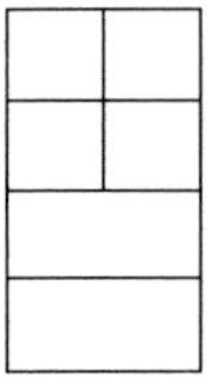

as:

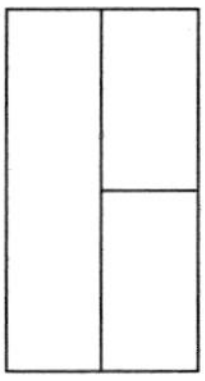

is to:

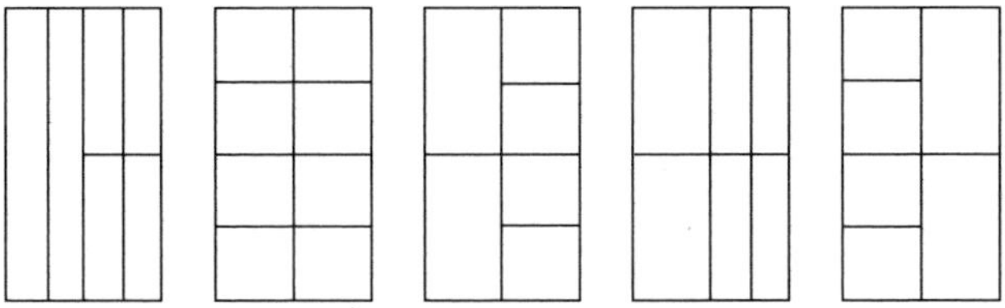

| A | B | C | D | E |

Answer [　　　]

31 Place the seven three-letter bits in the correct order to spell out a phrase.

ear, ewa, dis, for, for, med, rne

32

472	361	589
693	587	142
518	429	?

Which is the missing number?

A. 627

B. 981

C. 498

D. 367

E. 352

Answer

33 Which is the odd one out?

ramble, scurry, trudge, perambulate, march

34

14	19	5	30	48
11	2	24	6	8
15	21	4	10	16
13	9	39	18	32
3	7	17	12	1

Looking at straight lines horizontally, vertically or diagonally, what number is two places away from itself multiplied by 3, three places away from itself divided by 2 and three places away from itself plus 5?

Answer

35 What number is three times greater than 60 divided by a quarter?

Answer [ ]

36 If A = 3, B = 4, C = 5 and D = 6, calculate the following:

$$\frac{(A \times C) + (B \times D)}{(A \times B) + (D - C)}$$

Answer [ ]

37 What word can be placed in the brackets so that it forms another word or phrase when tacked on to the end of the first word, and another word or phrase when placed in front of the second word?

man (   ) red

38

4	5	7	3
8	3	3	9
7	6	9	5
6	9	8	?

What number should replace the question mark?

Answer [ ]

39 Which two words are closest in meaning?

pollinate, fervent, winsome, ecstatic, provoke, feverish

40

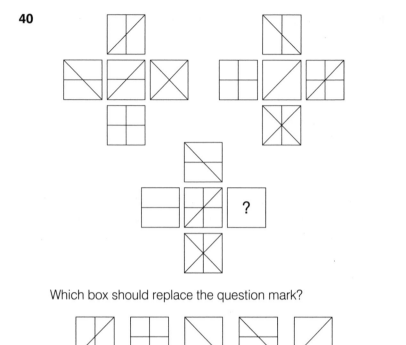

Which box should replace the question mark?

A   B   C   D   E

Answer

IQ test four

1

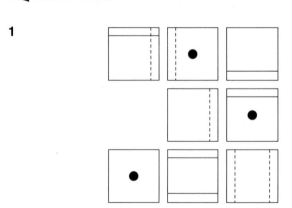

Draw the tile missing from the above matrix.

2   976 : 684

375 : 225

864 : 512

597 : ?

Answer [   ]

3   Alter one letter only from each word below to produce a familiar phrase.

AT TAR AN ORE CAT TALL

_____

4   Which two words are closest in meaning?

tumult, panoply, remedy, spectacle, contest, barricade

_____

5   If tax is charged at 22% on the first £55,000 and 35% on all income in excess of £55,000, how much tax is charged on an income of £80,000?

Answer [   ]

6

Which is the missing tile?

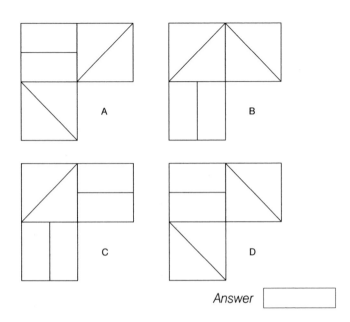

Answer [   ]

7 27, 54, ?, 108, 135, 162, 189, 216

What number is missing?

Answer

8 Combine three of the 10 three-letter bits to produce a word meaning GROUP.

ant, age, ain, ent, mer, ide, our, one, upi, lep

_____

9 Which is the odd one out?

busby, toque, cloche, sabot, biretta

_____

10

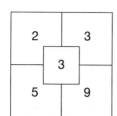 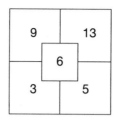

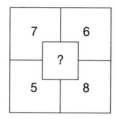

What number should replace the question mark?

Answer

11   A B C D E F G H

What letter is three to the left of the letter immediately to the right of the letter that is two to the left of the letter G?

Answer

12   ring is to rung as see is to: sees, seen, say, seeing

---

13   369, 121, 518, 212, 427, 303, ?

What three-digit number comes next?

Answer

14   D F R O I O N D ?

What letter is missing?

Answer

15 Which is the odd one out?

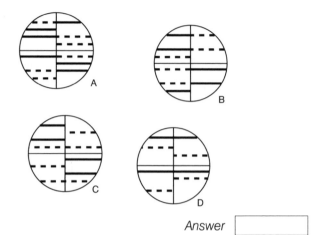

Answer [   ]

16 itinerary is to journey as agenda is to: boardroom, secretary, meeting, programme, minutes

_____

17 Which is the odd one out?

canyon, butte, ravine, gully, gorge

_____

18

A	C	F	H
D	F	I	K
F	H	K	M
I	K		

Which is the missing section?

N	Q
A

M	P
B

M	Q
C

N	P
D

Answer [   ]

19

Draw the missing pentagon in the above sequence.

20   LARGE ROUT is an anagram of which nine-letter word?

_____

21   How many different sized circles appear below?

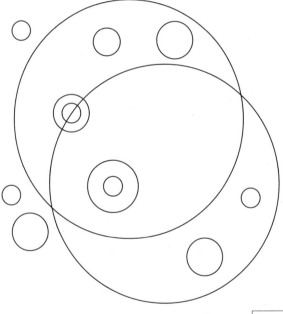

Answer [   ]

22   7 3 6
      8 9 7
      5 2 4
      6 7 ?

What number should replace the question mark?

Answer [   ]

23 The time is 24 minutes to the hour on a clock on which the numbers on the face are shown in Roman numerals. Arrange the numerals below in the order in which they appear from the minute hand reading anticlockwise.

XII II IX VI VIII IV

_____

24 72 (168) 96

35 (1112) 87

52 (610) 18

94 (?) 77

What number should replace the question mark?

Answer [   ]

25 DID TRUCE is an anagram of two 'this and that' words, CUT, DRIED (cut and dried). GIVE INK A LICK is an anagram of which two other 'this and that' words?

Clue: fit and well

_____

26 Which two words are most opposite in meaning?

feted, fractious, calm, genuine, durable, affable

_____

27

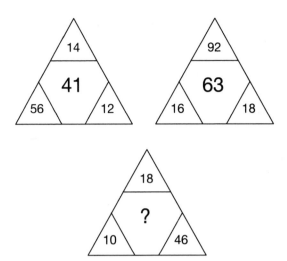

What number should replace the question mark?

Answer

28 Which word means the same as the definitions either side of the brackets?

in good health ( ) waterhole

29

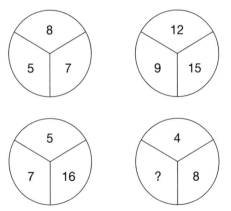

What number should replace the question mark?

Answer

30 What word can be placed in the brackets so that it forms another word or phrase when tacked on to the end of the first word, and another word or phrase when placed in front of the second word?

light (   ) book.

31 Prudence is one and a half times older than Patience, and Patience is one and a half times older than Charity. How old are Prudence, Patience and Charity if their combined ages total 133?

32

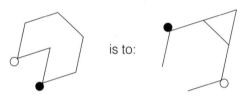

is to:

as:

is to:

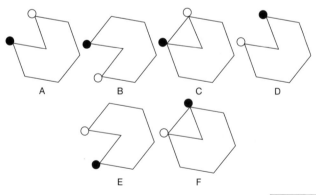

Answer

33 Place a word in the brackets that has the same meaning as the definitions either side of the brackets.

female deer (   ) posterior

34

3	8	5
6	2	8
5	6	?
1	7	?
7	4	?

What numbers should replace the question marks?

Answer [   ]

35 Only one group of five letters below can be rearranged to spell out a five-letter word in the English language. Identify the word.

AHLIN

WRDCO

FIONC

ARWON

DINCO

Answer [   ]

36

What number should replace the question mark?

Answer [   ]

37

3	18
22	?

14	?
9	10

15	2
6	18

What numbers should replace the question marks?

Answer

38 Identify two words (one from each set of brackets) that form a connection (analogy), thereby relating to the words in capitals in the same way.

LACTIC (vinegar, milk, apples)

CITRIC (vitamin, fruit, acid)

39

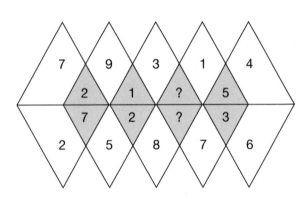

What numbers should replace the question marks?

Answer

40   SUNDAY

TUESDAY

FRIDAY

?

WEDNESDAY

FRIDAY

?

WEDNESDAY

SATURDAY

MONDAY

Which two days are missing?

_____

CHAPTER 5

Answers, explanations and assessments

Chapter 1

Test 1 General verbal aptitude test

Answers

1 previous
2 ordinary
3 believable
4 recurrent, frequent
5 formless, irregular
6 propitious, fortunate
7 inflame
8 allow
9 dissuade
10 meteoric, gradual
11 traumatic, relaxing

12   recant, maintain
13   susceptible, immune
14   litre (it is a measure of capacity; the rest are measures of length)
15   salutation (it is a welcome; the rest are farewells)
16   prologue (it is at the beginning; the rest are at the end)
17   transitory (it is temporary; the rest are permanent)
18   entrepreneur (it is an individual; the rest are companies)
19   carmine (it is red; the rest are shades of brown)
20   exacerbate
21   vegetation, animals
22   furthest, nearest
23   rectangle, ellipse
24   bud, leaf
25   analogous
26   need / knead
27   plight
28   cross
29   estimable
30   ordinance

Assessment

Score 1 point for each completely correct answer.

Total score	Rating	Percentage of population
28–30	Genius level	Top 5%
25–27	High expert	Top 10%
22–24	Expert	Top 30%
19–21	High average	Top 40%
15–18	Middle average	Top 60%
12–14	Low average	Bottom 40%
9–11	Borderline low	Bottom 30%
6–8	Low	Bottom 10%
0–5	Very low	Bottom 5%

Test 2 Word meanings test

Answers

1	a type of coarse cloth	canvas
	to solicit votes	canvass
2	noun: one who depends	dependant
	adjective: depending on	dependent
3	in that place	there
	belonging to them	their
4	impartial, unbiased	disinterested
	lacking interest	uninterested
5	unbroken, connected	continuous
	frequent, repeated	continual
6	verb: to give an opinion	advise
	noun: opinion given	advice
7	how much?	amount
	how many?	number
8	verb: to predict	prophesy
	noun: prediction	prophecy
9	very small or unimportant	negligible
	careless	negligent
10	unwilling, reluctant	loath
	dislike intensely	loathe
11	making less dark	lightening
	discharge of electricity in atmosphere	lightning
12	spirit of fortitude or endurance	morale
	of good conduct	moral
13	verb: to bring about; noun: result	effect
	verb: to act on, to influence	affect
14	every two years	biennial
	twice a year	bi-annual
15	notice or point out likenesses	compare
	notice or point out differences	contrast

16	body of water or electricity	current
	small berry	currant
17	to hint	imply
	to deduce or conclude	infer
18	stated in detail	explicit
	implied but not expressed	implicit
19	impending, close at hand	imminent
	abiding in, inherent	immanent
20	staff employed	personnel
	individual, private	personal
21	smaller in amount	less
	smaller in number	fewer
22	to inform	apprise
	to evaluate	appraise
23	that which completes	complement
	commendation, praise	compliment
24	faulty, incomplete	defective
	falling short	deficient
25	to turn aside, divert	distract
	to take away from	detract
26	more than ordinary	especially
	for a special occasion	specially
27	naïve, innocent	ingenuous
	cleverly contrived	ingenious
28	related to a judge, impartial	judicial
	sensible, prudent	judicious
29	examples	precedents
	priority	precedence
30	work with another	collaborate
	confirm, support a statement	corroborate

Assessment

Score 1 point for each completely correct answer.

Total score	Rating	Percentage of population
28–30	Genius level	Top 5%
25–27	High expert	Top 10%
22–24	Expert	Top 30%
19–21	High average	Top 40%
15–18	Middle average	Top 60%
12–14	Low average	Bottom 40%
9–11	Borderline low	Bottom 30%
6–8	Low	Bottom 10%
0–5	Very low	Bottom 5%

Test 3 Grammar and comprehension

Answers

1   As a craftsman he was extremely adept at creating artistic designs of metalwork and he was able to adopt his son's suggestion to adapt several of these creations, which enables them to be put to better use.

2   d

3   b

4   b

5   b

6   d

7   Quite a number of fish can give electric shocks to other animals, but in most that capacity is not very highly developed, serving rather as a warning than as a weapon.

8   Most plants, from large trees to tiny herbs, have branching roots.

9   For hundreds of years anagram compilers have tried to find hidden meanings in rearranging the names of famous people.

10   One of the problems with the use of abbreviations is that they are often only understood by the person who has used them and are, thus, not a very effective means of communication.

11   Good mathematical ability is an excellent stepping stone to career success in jobs such as accounting or banking.

12   It is extremely satisfying to have, or develop, the ability to take what at first glance may seem a difficult problem and, after unravelling the complications, arrive at a solution.

13   Sudoku puzzles are purely exercises in logic and no mathematical knowledge is necessary in order to solve them.

14   Brackets are generally used to enclose words that are not directly relevant to the main topic of the sentence.

15   The bombardier beetle, when attacked, emits from its posterior a volatile fluid which turns into gas when it comes in contact with the air.

Assessment

Score 1 point for each completely correct answer.

Total score	Rating	Percentage of population
14–15	Genius level	Top 5%
13	High expert	Top 10%
11–12	Expert	Top 30%
10	High average	Top 40%
8–9	Middle average	Top 60%
7	Low average	Bottom 40%
5–6	Borderline low	Bottom 30%
3–4	Low	Bottom 10%
0–2	Very low	Bottom 5%

Test 4 *Advanced verbal aptitude test*

Answers

1 b

2 d

3 profit and loss

4 stars and stripes

5 acquiesce

6 punctuate

7 A NOBLE CAR = Barcelona

The countries are Thailand (A THIN LAD), Malaysia (ALAS I MAY), Colombia (OIL A COMB), Bangladesh (BAG HANDLES).

8 occupational

9 troubleshoot

10 hold at bay

11 go too far

12 sit on the fence

13 complete, entire

14 succinct, rambling

15 HWTCA = watch

16 personify, represent

17 banging my head against a brick wall

18 terse nurse

19 pinion, spinal, supine, pippin

XYZ = PIN

20 strength, weakness

21 spearhead, forefront

22 holier-than-thou

23 sooner or later

24 word

All words can be prefixed with PASS to produce another word: passage, passable, passport, password.

25 eavesdropper

26 confound, bewilder

27 by all means

This produces: hub, may, tea, ail, nil, rim, hue, pea, ton, has.

28 exuberant, delighted

29

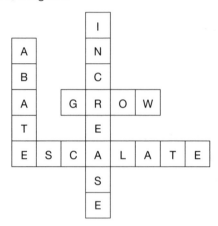

Synonyms: escalate, increase, grow

Antonym: abate

30 R

stain – strain

Assessment

Score 1 point for each completely correct answer.

Total score	Rating	Percentage of population
27–30	Genius level	Top 5%
24–26	High expert	Top 10%
20–23	Expert	Top 30%
16–19	High average	Top 40%
13–15	Middle average	Top 60%
11–12	Low average	Bottom 40%
8–10	Borderline low	Bottom 30%
4–7	Low	Bottom 10%
0–3	Very low	Bottom 5%

Chapter 2

Test 1 General spatial aptitude test

Answers

1   D

The rest are the same figure rotated.

2   A

The long hand moves 90° clockwise at each stage, and the short hand moves 45° anticlockwise.

3   C

The same three symbols are being repeated, starting at the top right-hand corner and working along the top line, then back along the next line, etc.

4   D

The slanting line moves two forward one back, the white dot moves three forward two back, the horizontal line moves two back one forward and the large circle moves two back one forward.

5   B

It contains three white dots and two black. The rest contain three black dots and two white.

6   C

Looking across and down, when two dots of the same colour appear in the same position in the first two squares they are carried forward to the third square, but then change from black to white and vice versa.

7   B

In all the others the same sequence of figures appears. In B the position of two of the figures is reversed.

8   B

A new dot is added until all dots have changed colour (which they do at each stage). The dots then disappear one at a time from the top, still changing colour.

9   C

The remainder are in pairs (A/E and B/D) in which the pattern on the outside is repeated on the inside.

10   D

It is the only one where the dot does not appear in the circle.

11   D

Only when lines appear in the same position in just two of the first three hexagons are they then transferred to the final hexagon.

12   E

Only when two elements appear in the same position in the first two squares, both across and down, are they transferred to the end square.

13   B

A new dot is added to the vertical and horizontal lines at each stage, and the dots appear black/white in turn.

14   D

The dot visits a different corner at each stage working clockwise and alternates black/white.

15   E

The rest are the same figure rotated.

16   C

The dots are moving from corner to corner so that in each line across and down they appear in four different corners.

17   D

Each connected line of four circles contains the four different symbols.

18   12

All the rest are in identical pairs but with black/white reversal: 1/9, 2/10, 3/5, 4/14, 6/13, 7/11, 8/15

19   E

Look at each line across and down. One small circle is empty; one contains a horizontal line and one a vertical line. One large circle is empty; one contains a horizontal line and one a vertical line. One square is empty and the other two contain opposite diagonal lines.

20   B

Each row across and down contains a line in each of the four different positions.

Assessment

Score 1 point for each correct answer.

Total score	Rating	Percentage of population
19–20	Genius level	Top 5%
17–18	High expert	Top 10%
15–16	Expert	Top 30%
13–14	High average	Top 40%
11–12	Middle average	Top 60%
9–10	Low average	Bottom 40%
7–8	Borderline low	Bottom 30%
5–6	Low	Bottom 10%
0–4	Very low	Bottom 5%

Test 2 Logical analysis test

Answers

1 D

The contents of box 1 plus the contents of box 2 equal the contents of box 3.

2 D

The contents of box 1 plus the contents of box 2 equal the contents of box 3.

3 C

The contents of box 1 plus the contents of box 2 equal the contents of box 3.

4 C

The contents of box 1 plus the contents of box 2 equal the contents of box 3.

5 A

The contents of box 1 plus the contents of box 2 equal the contents of box 3. However, like dots are cancelled out.

6 A

The contents of box 1 plus the contents of box 2 equal the contents of box 3. However, only lines that are common are carried forward.

7 E

The contents of box 1 plus the contents of box 2 equal the contents of box 3. However, when the same-colour dot appears in the same position in boxes 1 and 2 it changes from black to white and vice versa.

8 C

The contents of box 1 plus the contents of box 2 equal the contents of box 3. However, lines that are common are cancelled out.

9 B

The contents of box 1 plus the contents of box 2 equal the contents of box 3. However, lines that are common are cancelled out.

10 C

The contents of box 1 plus the contents of box 2 equal the contents of box 3. However, when a particular square or circle is common to both these boxes it changes from a square to a circle and vice versa.

Assessment

Each correct answer score 1 point.

Total score	Rating	Percentage of population
9–10	Genius level	Top 5%
8	High expert	Top 10%
7	Expert	Top 30%
6	High average	Top 40%
5	Middle average	Top 60%
4	Low average	Bottom 40%
3	Borderline low	Bottom 30%
2	Low	Bottom 10%
0–1	Very low	Bottom 5%

Test 3 Advanced matrix test

Answers

1   Tile 1B is incorrect and should be replaced by tile D.

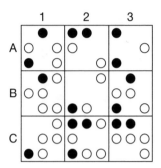

2   Tile 3B is incorrect and should be replaced by tile C.

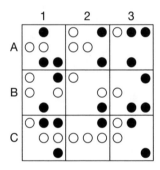

3   Tile 1B is incorrect and should be replaced by tile E.

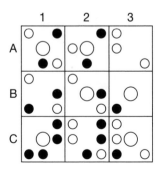

4 Tile 2A is incorrect and should be replaced by tile A.

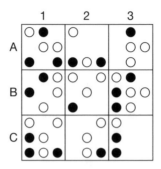

5 Tile 2B is incorrect and should be replaced by tile B.

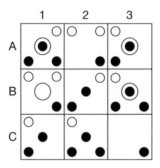

6 Tile 1C is incorrect and should be replaced by tile D.

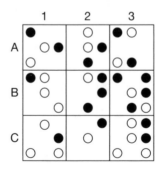

7   Tile 3C is incorrect and should be replaced by tile A.

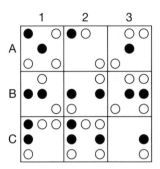

8   Tile 2A is incorrect and should be replaced by tile C.

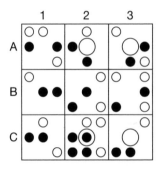

9   Tile 2C is incorrect and should be replaced by tile E.

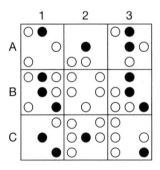

10 Tile 1B is incorrect and should be replaced by tile D.

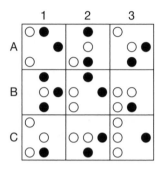

Assessment

Each correct answer score 1 point.

Total score	Rating	Percentage of population
9–10	Genius level	Top 5%
8	High expert	Top 10%
7	Expert	Top 30%
6	High average	Top 40%
5	Middle average	Top 60%
4	Low average	Bottom 40%
3	Borderline low	Bottom 30%
2	Low	Bottom 10%
0–1	Very low	Bottom 5%

Chapter 3

Test 1 Mental arithmetic

Answers

1	72	**7**	150	**13**	79	**19**	508	**25**	207
2	89	**8**	300	**14**	85	**20**	9	**26**	1434
3	209	**9**	199	**15**	148	**21**	54	**27**	539
4	128	**10**	225	**16**	52.5	**22**	1613	**28**	0.75
5	24	**11**	62	**17**	855	**23**	1368	**29**	72
6	19	**12**	120	**18**	48	**24**	62.5	**30**	3

Assessment

Score 1 point for each completely correct answer above.

Total score	Rating	Percentage of population
28–30	Genius level	Top 5%
25–27	High expert	Top 10%
22–24	Expert	Top 30%
19–21	High average	Top 40%
15–18	Middle average	Top 60%
12–14	Low average	Bottom 40%
9–11	Borderline low	Bottom 30%
6–8	Low	Bottom 10%
0–5	Very low	Bottom 5%

Test 2 Numerical sequence test

Answers

1   22
Add 1, 1, 1, 2, 2, 2, 3, 3, 3, 4.

2   48
Add 3, 6, 9, 12, 15.

3   625
Deduct 25, 50, 75, 100, 125.

4   5.5, 2.5
There are two interwoven sequences: starting at 1 add 1.5; starting at 10 deduct 2.5.

5   –2
Deduct 3.5 at each stage.

6   4096
×2, ×4 repeated

7   –3
–1, –2, –3, –4, –5

8   61.5
The amount added on is multiplied by 3 each time, ie 0.5, 1.5, 4.5, 13.5, 40.5.

9   279
×3, +3 repeated.

10   19, 36
There are two interwoven sequences: starting at 5 add 2, 3, 4, 5; starting at 6 add 2, 4, 8, 16.

11   51
Deduct 1, 3, 5, 7, 9, 11, 13.

12   133
Add 19 each time.

13   248
×2+1, ×2+2, ×2+3, ×2+4, ×2+5, ×2+6

14   4.75
–0.25, –0.5, –0.75, –1, –1.25, –1.5

15   10.25
+1.75, –2.5, +1.75, –2.5, +1.75

Assessment

Score 1 point for each correct answer.

Total score	Rating	Percentage of population
14–15	Genius level	Top 5%
13	High expert	Top 10%
11–12	Expert	Top 30%
10	High average	Top 40%
8–9	Middle average	Top 60%
7	Low average	Bottom 40%
5–6	Borderline low	Bottom 30%
3–4	Low	Bottom 10%
0–2	Very low	Bottom 5%

Test 3 Working with numbers

Answers

1 4

2 72165

3 C

Looking across, the numbers progress +2, +3, +2, +3.
Looking down, they progress +3, +2, +3, +2.

4 36

5 8

72 ÷ 9

6

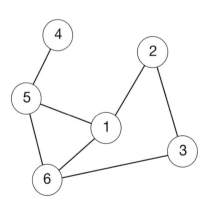

7

3	×	8	÷	6	=	4
+	■	−	■	+	■	+
2	+	3	+	3	=	8
−	■	−	■	÷	■	÷
3	−	1	×	3	=	6
=	■	=	■	=	■	=
2	+	4	÷	3	=	2

8 £60.00   £100.00   originally
      £40.00   £120.00   Phil to Jill
      £80.00   £80.00   Jill to Phil

9 2/3
      3/8 × 16/9

10 A

11 1008
      16 × 63

12 41
      Total 197

13 Jo 16, Mo 11, Flo 22

14 44
      (5 × 7) + 9

15 16
      Product = 672

16

7	3	1
5	6	4
9	2	8

17 18

A = 3, B = 6, C = 5, D = 10

18 35°

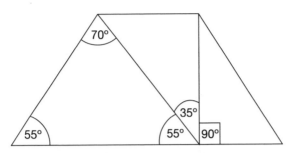

The three angles in a triangle always total 180°.

Angle y = 180 – (70 + 55) = 55

Angle z = 90° (a right angle)

The three angles on a straight line = 180°.

Therefore angle x = 180 – (55 + 90).

19

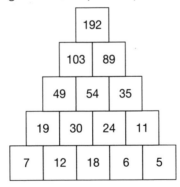

20 Harry = 138, Barry = 69

Assessment

Score 1 point for each correct answer.

Total score	Rating	Percentage of population
19–20	Genius level	Top 5%
17–18	High expert	Top 10%
15–16	Expert	Top 30%
13–14	High average	Top 40%
11–12	Middle average	Top 60%
9–10	Low average	Bottom 40%
7–8	Borderline low	Bottom 30%
5–6	Low	Bottom 10%
0–4	Very low	Bottom 5%

Test 4 Numerical problem solving

Answers

1 9

$9 \times 8 = 72$; $72 - 63 = 9$

2 12

4×3

3 10

$10 + 2 = 12$

$10 - 4 = 6$

4 She starts with £240.00

First store $240 - (120 + 20) = 100$

Second store $100 - (50 + 10) = 40$

Third store $40 - (20 + 20) = 0$

5 37 minutes

12 noon – 37 minutes = 11.23

11.23 less 32 minutes = 10.51

9 am plus 111 minutes $(37 \times 3) = 10.51$

6 220

Now $208 - (4 \times 4) = 192$

In seven years' time $192 + (4 \times 7) = 220$

7 £60.00

Mo 5/8 $=$ 37.50

Jo 0.25 $=$ 15.00

Flo $\underline{\quad 7.50}$

$\overline{60.00}$

8 Minus £32.50

£180 × 5/9 $=$ £100.00

£180.00 × 0.375 $=$ £67.50

Cheque $\underline{\quad £45.00}$

$\overline{£212.50}$

9 576 boxes

Capacity of box = 288 cu metres ($8 \times 6 \times 6$)

Each box = 0.5 cu metres ($1 \times 1 \times 0.5$)

10 1250

$(175 \div 14) \times 100$

11 5

3 numbers = $29 \times 3 = 87$

2 numbers = $41 \times 2 = 82$

The third number must, therefore, be 5 ($87 - 82$).

12 2 minutes 15 seconds

$(2.5 + 0.5) \times \dfrac{60}{80}$

13 1 hour 31 minutes

$28 + 28 + 35$

14 240 grapefruit, 320 oranges and 160 pears

$720 \div 9$ ($3 + 4 + 2$) $=$ 80

grapefruit = 3×80 $=$ 240

oranges = 4×80 $=$ 320

pears = 2×80 $=$ $\underline{160}$

$\overline{720}$

15 £2.50

A pack costs £2.76 or £0.46 each in the pack. If bought individually they cost £0.50 (4 pence more).

£0.50 × 5 = £2.50

Assessment

Score 1 point for each correct answer.

Total score	Rating	Percentage of population
14–15	Genius level	Top 5%
13	High expert	Top 10%
11–12	Expert	Top 30%
10	High average	Top 40%
8–9	Middle average	Top 60%
7	Low average	Bottom 40%
5–6	Borderline low	Bottom 30%
3–4	Low	Bottom 10%
0–2	Very low	Bottom 5%

Chapter 4

IQ test one

Answers

1   A

The dot and shaded portion are each in three circles. In the rest they are in two.

2   healthy

3   bank

4   21, 31

There are two interwoven sequences. Start at the first 1 and add 2, 3, 4, 5, 6. Start at the second 1 and add 2, 4, 6, 8, 10.

5   16 per minute

Between 2 pm and 3 pm 600 enquiries were received. There were 60% more between 3 pm and 4 pm, ie 960, which is 16 (960/60) per minute.

6   12

The numbers in each segment plus the number in the circle attached to it always total 20, ie 5 + 3 + 12 = 20, 3 + 7 + 10 = 20, etc.

7 A

Looking across numbers progress −1, +2, −1, +2. Looking down they progress −2, +1, −2, +1.

8 bold, intrepid

9 B

Looking across and down, only circles that are common to the first two squares are carried forward to the end square. However, they then change from black to white and vice versa.

10 stratosphere

11 apricot, pear, cherry

12 paper

13 E

The contents of each hexagon are determined by the contents of the two hexagons immediately below it. Lines from these two hexagons are carried forward to the hexagon above, except when two lines appear in the same position, in which case they are cancelled out.

14 tawdry, graceful

15 9417

Numbers are in pairs where the digits swap round ABCD/ CBDA, ie 7491/9417, 7183/8137, 2639/3692, 5826/2865.

16 philander

17

7	9	4	2
6	3	8	1
5	2	6	9
4	7	3	5

6	8	5	3
7	2	9	0
4	3	7	8
5	6	2	4

Looking from the left square to the right square, the odd numbers are −1 and the even numbers +1.

18 BULL MARE = umbrella

The animals are gazelle (LEG ZEAL), orang-utan (GAUNT RONA), elephant (THE PANEL) and gorilla (LOG RAIL).

19 A

20 E

21 B

Looking across, progress three letters in the alphabet then four letters. Looking down, progress five letters then four.

22

	Now	+4 years	−3 years
Angela	24	28	21
Barry	10	14	7
Carol	3	7	

23 congeal

It means to harden; the rest are to soften.

24 C

The two sets, when added together, produce three complete circles.

25 4163 and 7496

26 quality

Each word commences with the last letter of the previous word plus two places in the alphabet, and each word increases by one letter in length.

27 2

The number formed by the second two digits in each line is half of the number formed by the first two digits, eg 72/36.

28 stream

29 sleep, eat

30 C

Superimpose the two figures and change circles to crosses and vice versa.

31 32

32 melodramatic

33 hypotenuse

It is the line in a triangle; the rest are lines in circles.

34 607

×3 +1 at each stage

35 12

36 circle

37 40%

Average age is 35 (350/10)

38 peak / pique

39 27

Alternate numbers in each column total 100.

40

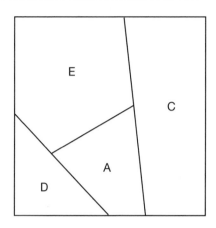

Assessment

Score 1 point for each correct answer.

Total score	Rating	Percentage of population
37–40	Genius level	Top 5%
32–36	High expert	Top 10%
28–31	Expert	Top 30%
24–27	High average	Top 40%
17–23	Middle average	Top 60%
13–16	Low average	Bottom 40%
9–12	Borderline low	Bottom 30%
5–8	Low	Bottom 10%
0–4	Very low	Bottom 5%

IQ test two

Answers

1   E

Lines continue from adjacent squares. However, continuous lines become broken and vice versa.

2   monumental

3   3

397 × 2 = 794, 249 × 2 = 498, 168 × 2 = 336, ie the numbers formed by the first three digits on each row are half the value of the numbers formed by the last three digits on each row, albeit in the wrong order.

4   windpipe

5   9

62 × 8 = 496; similarly 49 × 3 = 147 and 75 × 5 = 375

6   917

4 + 5 = 9 and 8 + 9 = 17

7   16 in both lines

7 × 4 = 28 and 2 × 8 = 16

8   env(iron)ment

9   10

So the total of each line across, down and corner to corner is 30

10   increase, diminish

11   helicopter

It is an anagram of elite porch, and automobile is an anagram of ileum taboo.

12   Al 54, Sal 72, Mal 96

13   plot

14   1 metre

fence = 4 metres

15

Each line contains a heart, spade and club with one of the symbols inverted.

16 638952

Reverse the fifth and fourth digits; then take the remaining digits in order from right to left.

17 alpine, nettle, length, thirst, stigma, manual

18 5

$(6 + 14 + 10) \div 6$

19 refrain

20 unemotional

21 C

Only circles common to the first two squares in each line across and down are carried forward to the final square. However, they then change from white to black and vice versa.

22 E

In all the others a black dot is inside a figure with an odd number of sides and a white dot is inside a figure with an even number of sides.

23 Honesty is the Best Policy

24

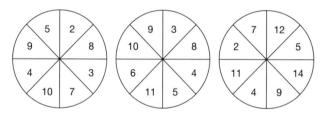

In the first circle opposite segments total 12, in the second circle they total 14 and in the third circle they total 16.

25 land

26 undoubtedly

27 7

Add 2¾ each time.

28

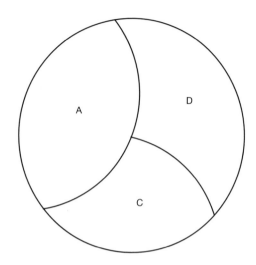

29   21

Divide each number in the corner by 7 and add to obtain the number in the centre.

30   S

31   ultimatum

32   fable

It is a story; the rest are sayings or proverbs.

33   9

$39^2 = 1521$

34   D

One is a mirror image of the other.

35   E

Looking across and down, add the white dots in the first two squares to obtain the number of white dots in the final square. For the black dots, subtract.

36   2.5

The amount deducted increases by 6.5 each time: 6.5, 13, 19.5, 26, 32.5.

37   Sunday 6 August

38   F

39   228

$(9 + 3) \times 19$

40   devise

Assessment

Score 1 point for each correct answer.

Total score	Rating	Percentage of population
37–40	Genius level	Top 5%
32–36	High expert	Top 10%
28–31	Expert	Top 30%
24–27	High average	Top 40%
17–23	Middle average	Top 60%
13–16	Low average	Bottom 40%
9–12	Borderline low	Bottom 30%
5–8	Low	Bottom 10%
0–4	Very low	Bottom 5%

IQ test three

Answers

1   A

The line moves 45° at each stage and alternates straight/ curved. The dot moves on the line top/middle/bottom and back again.

2   66, 35

There are two interwoven sequences. Start at 100 and deduct 8.5. Start at 1 and add 8.5.

3   bear, fox

4   8

The number at the top is the square root of the number formed by the two digits at the bottom, ie $\sqrt{81} = 9$.

5   E

The number of circles decreases by one each time, and one circle at each stage does not contain a dot.

6   F

Looking both across and down, lines are carried forward from the first two squares, except when two lines are in the same position in these two squares in which case they are cancelled out.

7   MEOPT = tempo

8   case

9   24

Looking across and down, the final number in each row and column is the sum of the first three numbers.

10   B

The left half of the complete array is a mirror image of the right half.

11   speed

12   educator

13   52413 or 31425

14   distribute

They all contain a body part: e(leg)ant, f(ear)less, mids(hip)man, el(lip)tical, hackn(eye)d, dist(rib)ute.

15   A

Looking across and down, the white dot moves one corner clockwise at each stage. Looking across, the black line moves 45° clockwise and the dotted line 90° anticlockwise. Looking down, the black line moves 45° anticlockwise and the dotted line 90° clockwise.

16   5

19 + 26 = 45; similarly 5 + 9 = 14 and 17 + 11 = 28

17   ABDGKP

Miss an extra letter in the alphabet each time: ABcDefGhijKlmnoP.

18   d

19   A

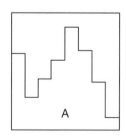

20 6897

Start at 7492836 and working anticlockwise reverse each number and omit the smallest digit.

21 1 hour 53 minutes (113 minutes)

22 as plain as day

23 124

384/768 = ½; ½² = ¼; 496 × ¼ = 124

24 portfolio

25 Sally is now 14.

26 D

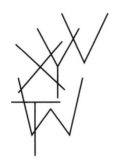

It contains the letters T V W X Y, which omits the letter U. The rest contain five consecutive letters of the alphabet.

27 in real life

28 4

(4 × 16) ÷ (2 × 8)

29 chaste

30 C

Every section is divided into two halves by a horizontal line.

31 forewarned is forearmed

32 d

367: so that each row and column contains the digits 1 to 9 once each only.

33 scurry

It is a form of running. The rest are forms of walking.

34 2

35 720

36 3

37 kind

38 8

The sum of the numbers in each line across increases by 4.

39 fervent, ecstatic

40 A

Each row and column of three boxes contains two of each of the three different lines, ie horizontal, vertical and diagonal.

Assessment

Score 1 point for each correct answer.

Total score	Rating	Percentage of population
37–40	Genius level	Top 5%
32–36	High expert	Top 10%
28–31	Expert	Top 30%
24–27	High average	Top 40%
17–23	Middle average	Top 60%
13–16	Low average	Bottom 40%
9–12	Borderline low	Bottom 30%
5–8	Low	Bottom 10%
0–4	Very low	Bottom 5%

IQ test four

Answers

1

Each line across and down contains a complete line top and bottom, a broken line left and right and a black dot.

2   485

5×97

3   as far as one can tell

4   panoply, spectacle

5   £20850

22% of £55000	=	£12100
35% of £25000	=	£8750
£80000		£20850

6   B

Each line and column contains one each of the four different lines.

7   81

Add 27 each time.

8   entourage

9   sabot

It is footwear; the rest are headwear.

10   26

$(7 \times 8) - (5 \times 6)$

11   C

12   seen

13   336

It is the three times table split into groups of three numbers: 3, 6, 9, 12, 15, 18, 21, 24, 27, 30, 33, 36.

14   K

The words FOOD and DRINK are spelled out by alternate letters.

15   B

In all the others, diagonally opposite segments have the same arrangement of lines.

16   meeting

17   butte

It is a hill; the rest are ravines or valleys.

18   D

Looking across, miss one then two letters of the alphabet. Looking down, miss two then one.

19

Add another triangle at each stage with its base on a different side of the pentagon working clockwise.

20 regulator

21 5

22 2

$6 \times 7 = 42$

23 VI, IV, II, XII, IX, VIII

24 1611

$9 + 7 = 16$ and $4 + 7 = 11$

25 alive and kicking

26 fractious, affable

27 37

Divide each number in the corner by 2 and add to obtain the number in the centre.

28 well

29 4

$(8 + 4) \div 3$

30 year

31 Charity 28, Patience 42, Prudence 63

32 D

The projecting point moves to the opposite inside position. The dots move to the other end of the line and change from black to white and vice versa.

33 hind

34 7

3

9

Reverse the numbers and add 1.

35 WRDCO = crowd

36 41

$(7 \times 8) - 15$

37

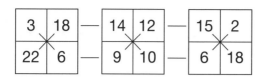

The numbers produce two sequences as indicated above, ie:

3, 6, 9, 12, 15, 18

22, 18, 14, 10, 6, 2

38 milk, fruit

39 4

7

Looking at adjacent numbers in the larger sections, $7 - 3 = 4$ and $8 - 1 = 7$.

40 SUNDAY

MONDAY

The sequence progresses miss one day and then miss two days alternately.

Assessment

Score 1 point for each correct answer.

Total score	Rating	Percentage of population
37–40	Genius level	Top 5%
32–36	High expert	Top 10%
28–31	Expert	Top 30%
24–27	High average	Top 40%
17–23	Middle average	Top 60%
13–16	Low average	Bottom 40%
9–12	Borderline low	Bottom 30%
5–8	Low	Bottom 10%
0–4	Very low	Bottom 5%

With over 1,000 titles in printed and digital format, **Kogan Page** offers affordable, sound business advice

www.koganpage.com